Digital Asset Management

2024 Edition

By Greg Kihlström

Copyright © 2024 by Greg Kihlström.

All rights reserved. In accordance with the US Copyright Act of 1976, the scanning, uploading, and electronic sharing of any part of this book without the permission of the publisher constitutes unlawful piracy and theft of the author's intellectual property. If you would like to use material from the book (other than for review purposes), prior written permission must be obtained by contacting the author. Thank you for your support of the author's rights.

Published by:

Agile Brand, LLC

3100 Clarendon Boulevard #200

Arlington, VA 22201

https://www.gregkihlstrom.com

First Edition: December 2024

The publisher is not responsible for websites (or their content) that are not owned by the publisher.

Cover design and illustrations by Greg Kihlström

ISBN: 9798345413999

Contents

ACKNOWLEDGEMENTS 7

INTRODUCTION 9

PART 1: MAKING THE BUSINESS CASE FOR A DAM 13

CHAPTER 1: UNDERSTANDING THE ROLE OF DAM IN MARKETING SUCCESS 15

CHAPTER 2: KEY BUSINESS BENEFITS OF IMPLEMENTING A DAM 22

CHAPTER 3: BUILDING A STRONG BUSINESS CASE FOR DAM INVESTMENT 32

PART 2: CORE AND ADVANCED FEATURES OF A DAM 42

CHAPTER 4: CORE FEATURES EVERY DAM SHOULD HAVE 44

CHAPTER 5: ADVANCED FEATURES THAT SET A DAM APART 54

CHAPTER 6: LEVERAGING AI IN DAM SYSTEMS 65

PART 3: EVALUATING AND CHOOSING THE RIGHT DAM 75

CHAPTER 7: IDENTIFYING STAKEHOLDERS AND ASSEMBLING A TEAM FOR EVALUATION 77

CHAPTER 8: DEVELOPING A SELECTION CRITERIA AND EVALUATION FRAMEWORK 87

CHAPTER 9: CONDUCTING DEMOS AND TRIAL RUNS 97

PART 4: IMPLEMENTING A DAM 107

CHAPTER 10: PLANNING FOR IMPLEMENTATION 109

CHAPTER 11: CONFIGURING YOUR DAM TO MAXIMIZE EFFICIENCY   119

CHAPTER 12: TRAINING AND ONBOARDING YOUR TEAM   128

PART 5: BEST PRACTICES FOR ONGOING USAGE AND OPTIMIZATION   138

CHAPTER 13: ESTABLISHING DAM GOVERNANCE AND USAGE GUIDELINES   140

CHAPTER 14: INTEGRATING DAM WITH YOUR MARKETING TECHNOLOGY STACK   151

CHAPTER 15: MEASURING SUCCESS AND CONTINUOUSLY OPTIMIZING YOUR DAM   161

PART 6: FUTURE-PROOFING YOUR DAM INVESTMENT   171

CHAPTER 16: KEEPING UP WITH DAM TRENDS AND INNOVATIONS   173

CHAPTER 17: PREPARING FOR THE FUTURE OF CONTENT AND DAM   182

CHAPTER 18: EMERGING DAM USE CASES AND WHAT MARKETERS SHOULD EXPECT   192

EPILOGUE   202

APPENDIX 1: DAM EVALUATION CHECKLIST   204

APPENDIX 2: GLOSSARY OF DIGITAL ASSET MANAGEMENT (DAM) TERMS   210

To Lindsey,

my partner in agility.

Also by Greg Kihlström:

The Agile Series:

- *The Agile Brand* (new edition 2025 - forthcoming)

Priority is Action Series:

- *Priority is Action* (2024)
- *Priority is Prediction* (2024)

House of the Customer Series:

- *The Center of Experience* (2020 and 2023)
- *Meaningful Measurement of the Customer Experience* (2023)
- *House of the Customer* (2023)

Agile Brand Guides:

- *Customer Data Platforms* (CDPs) (2024)
- *Customer Journey Orchestration Platforms* (2024)
- *Digital Experience Platforms* (2024)
- *Marketing Operations* (2023)
- *Conversational Marketing* (2023)
- *Generative AI* (2023)

The Composable Roadmap, with co-author Chad Solomonson (2024)

Acknowledgements

As with any book, countless people had a hand in the thoughts and ideas contained within. I will endeavor to thank many of them, but a full list would take up its own book, so please excuse this abbreviated list.

First, I want to thank the many amazing people I work with as an advisor and consultant. I have had the privilege and opportunity to experience many different ways of working, including working firsthand with many platforms, including Digital Asset Management platforms.

Thanks also to my wife Lindsey, who is always supportive of me, no matter how many books I write during the course of a year (this year, it will be three). She is forever an inspiration, and I'm thankful to have such a great partner in all things.

Finally, thank you to everyone reading this book and anyone who has listened to my podcast, read an article, and supported me in any way over the last several years. I hope that the thoughts and ideas shared by myself and others have been helpful in your work.

Let's move forward and create great things together!

Introduction

When "digital" is now the go-to mindset for many these days, marketers face unprecedented demand for high-quality, consistent, and personalized content across multiple channels. With consumer expectations at an all-time high, brands must deliver visually engaging experiences quickly and seamlessly—on websites, social media, email, apps, and beyond. Meeting this demand requires more than a collection of assets; it requires a system that brings organization, efficiency, and strategic insight to content management. This is where Digital Asset Management (DAM) comes into play.

DAM is the backbone of modern marketing, enabling teams to store, organize, find, and deploy assets effectively. With a well-implemented DAM system, marketers can reduce content production time, prevent redundancy, ensure brand consistency, and foster collaboration across departments. By centralizing assets and automating workflows, DAM empowers marketing teams to act quickly and strategically, allowing them to focus less on administrative tasks and more on creative initiatives that engage audiences and drive results. DAM isn't just a storage solution—it's a vital tool for enhancing productivity, improving brand coherence, and delivering memorable customer experiences.

This is based on research . . . and experience

My work continually informs my writing, and this book is an example of that. I have been privileged to work with several organizations of varying sizes (from Fortune 50 to 1000) and assisted with strategy creation, solution finding, and delivering many types of initiatives that the Agile approaches described in this book can help teams achieve. I am committed to being both a writer-researcher and a practitioner; I want my insights to be more than purely theoretical. My hope is that this makes the concepts on the page more actionable, insightful, and beneficial to you, the reader.

Who This Book Is For

This book is for marketing executives and professionals at primarily large organizations that need to quickly get up to speed on digital asset management as a practice as well as DAMs as a platform and understand them in the context of a broader marketing strategy. As much is riding on smart investments in a platform such as a DAM, it is critical that marketing leaders understand the details and implications that are involved in the decision to adopt a platform.

Also, this is a *guide,* not an *encyclopedia*; therefore, it is intended to be a short read and to quickly and easily give you a good understanding, though to get more in-depth knowledge, more reading, training, and experience will be required.

Objectives of the Book

This guide provides marketers with a comprehensive roadmap to implementing, managing, and maximizing the potential of a DAM system. Throughout this book, you will learn:

1. **Fundamentals and Best Practices**: Understand what DAM is, why it's essential for marketing, and how it can transform your team's approach to content. You'll learn best practices for organizing, tagging, and maintaining assets to ensure a streamlined and user-friendly system.
2. **Evaluating and Implementing DAM**: Discover how to evaluate DAM options, select a solution that aligns with your organization's goals, and implement it effectively. From setting up metadata and taxonomy to configuring workflows and permissions, this book provides actionable guidance for creating a scalable DAM that meets your specific needs.
3. **Advanced Strategies for DAM Optimization**: Explore advanced topics such as integrating DAM with your martech stack, automating personalization, and leveraging AI for content creation and adaptation. You'll learn how to turn DAM into a powerhouse

for supporting multi-channel marketing, dynamic content personalization, and real-time distribution.

4. **Future-Proofing Your DAM Strategy**: Gain insights into emerging trends in DAM, including shoppable assets, immersive experiences, and AI-driven content strategies. This guide prepares you for the next generation of digital marketing, ensuring that your DAM remains a competitive advantage as technology and customer expectations evolve.

Whether you're setting up a DAM from scratch, optimizing an existing system, or looking for ways to push the boundaries of what DAM can do, this book offers strategies to elevate your marketing efforts. By applying the principles in this guide, marketers will be equipped to drive efficiency, consistency, and impact—transforming DAM from a functional tool into a strategic asset that powers your brand's success.

Additional Resources

You can find some related resources, as mentioned within the chapters that follow, available on my website, https://gregkihlstrom.com/, or directly at https://agilebrandguides.com

Get in touch with me if you have any questions or would like to be pointed in the right direction.

Part 1: Making the Business Case for a DAM

Digital Asset Management (DAM) is increasingly becoming a foundational system for modern marketing teams. As the demand for high-quality, on-brand content continues to rise, so too does the need for efficient ways to manage these assets. However, gaining buy-in for DAM within an organization requires more than just explaining its technical benefits—it involves building a comprehensive business case that highlights DAM's role in driving efficiency, brand consistency, and measurable ROI. In this first part of the book, we'll explore how to effectively present the need for a DAM system to decision-makers and align it with the broader goals of your organization.

The chapters in Part 1 are designed to help you articulate the concrete benefits of DAM, including the operational efficiencies it offers, the potential for cost savings, and its impact on collaboration and speed to market. You'll learn how to quantify the time and financial costs associated with inefficient asset management and demonstrate how DAM can help mitigate these issues. By grounding your case in data and real-world examples, you'll be better equipped to secure the support of key stakeholders across departments, from marketing and creative to IT, legal, and finance.

Making the business case for DAM isn't just about securing budget approval—it's about positioning DAM as a strategic investment that will empower your marketing team to work more effectively and respond faster to market demands. Part 1 will guide you through identifying the problems a DAM system can solve, quantifying its value with meaningful metrics, and creating a step-by-step roadmap to implementation. With this foundation, you'll be ready to advocate for DAM not only as a solution to current challenges but as a driver of long-term growth and competitive advantage.

Chapter 1: Understanding the Role of DAM in Marketing Success

Explaining DAM's role in streamlining content workflows, brand consistency, and collaboration.

TL;DR

Digital Asset Management (DAM) is essential for today's marketers, providing a centralized, organized system for storing, managing, and retrieving digital assets. Modern DAM systems go beyond simple storage—they enhance marketing efficiency by saving time, improving brand consistency, and supporting agile, multi-channel campaigns. Key benefits include faster asset retrieval, streamlined collaboration across teams, and the ability to maintain a cohesive brand image. For marketers, a DAM transforms digital content into a strategic asset, empowering them to adapt quickly and deliver effective, on-brand campaigns across all channels.

In today's marketing landscape, where content reigns supreme, having control over your digital assets isn't just a luxury—it's a necessity. For marketers, content represents the essence of brand identity, the fuel for multi-channel campaigns, and the bridge to connect with consumers in a personalized, meaningful way. But managing and delivering this content effectively is challenging, especially as asset volume and complexity grow. This is where Digital Asset Management (DAM) systems come into play. DAM systems offer an organized, efficient way to store, manage, and retrieve digital assets, positioning them at the core of a successful marketing strategy.

In this chapter, we'll explore the purpose of DAM in modern marketing, its evolution from basic storage solutions to essential marketing tools, and the transformative impact it can have on teams by enhancing collaboration, brand consistency, and workflow efficiency.

1.1 The Growing Importance of Digital Assets in Marketing

In today's digital-first world, brands are communicating across more platforms than ever—social media, websites, email campaigns, video channels, and beyond. This omnichannel approach requires a vast library of digital assets: images, videos, documents, graphics, and more. The sheer volume of content necessary to reach consumers across different touchpoints demands a solution that can handle large quantities of assets, provide quick retrieval, and ensure proper usage.

Digital assets serve as a brand's visual and textual language, making them invaluable to marketing. Whether it's a product photo, promotional video, or an infographic for a blog post, these assets need to be readily accessible, high-quality, and aligned with brand guidelines. By centralizing all digital assets, DAM systems eliminate silos and simplify the asset retrieval process, ultimately allowing marketers to focus more on strategic creativity than on operational logistics.

Example: The Cost of Asset Mismanagement

Consider a global brand launching a product across multiple regions. Without an effective DAM, marketers in each region may use outdated logos, miss approved templates, or spend hours searching for the right imagery. This lack of coordination leads to inconsistent brand representation, delays, and resource wastage. A DAM mitigates these issues by centralizing approved assets, making it easy for global teams to stay aligned.

1.2 Evolution of DAM: From Storage to Strategic Marketing Tool

DAM systems have evolved significantly from their early days as simple media storage solutions. Originally, DAM was often relegated to the IT department, viewed merely as a storage and retrieval system for digital files. But as marketing needs became more complex, DAM transformed into a dynamic tool essential for brand consistency, content delivery, and marketing agility.

Today's DAM platforms are designed specifically for marketers. They incorporate advanced features, such as metadata tagging, AI-driven search capabilities, and integration with other marketing tools like content management systems (CMS) and customer relationship management (CRM) platforms. Modern DAM systems don't just store assets; they enable a strategic approach to managing the lifecycle of content—tracking it from creation through to publication and eventual retirement.

Key Features in Modern DAM Systems

- **Metadata and Tagging**: This feature allows marketers to tag assets with keywords, descriptions, and categories, making search faster and retrieval more accurate.
- **AI-Powered Search**: Advanced DAM platforms use artificial intelligence to help locate assets based on keywords, visual recognition, or context.

- **Integration with Martech Stack**: DAMs now integrate with tools like CMS, project management platforms, and analytics tools, streamlining workflows and ensuring consistency across channels.

1.3 How DAM Enhances Marketing Efficiency and Agility

With DAM, marketers gain control over the lifecycle of their assets, from creation to final delivery. DAM solutions enable a more agile marketing team, allowing quicker campaign rollouts, efficient collaboration, and faster adaptation to market changes. Here's how:

- **Time Savings**: DAM eliminates time wasted searching for assets by providing a centralized, searchable library of approved content. This streamlined access can reduce asset retrieval time by as much as 40%, according to recent industry reports.
- **Improved Collaboration**: With DAM, teams across marketing, creative, and sales have a single source of truth for approved assets, minimizing errors and ensuring brand consistency. Real-time access allows remote teams to collaborate without version conflicts or delays.
- **Enhanced Brand Consistency**: DAM acts as the gatekeeper for brand assets, ensuring that only approved content, logos, and templates are available to teams, thus maintaining a consistent brand image across all marketing channels.

Example: Agility in Action with DAM

Imagine a scenario where a new product launch campaign needs to be adjusted to accommodate a sudden shift in market trends. With a DAM, marketers can quickly locate, adjust, and deploy relevant assets without delay. This agility is especially important in digital channels, where timely updates can make or break a campaign.

1.4 DAM as a Driver for Multi-Channel Marketing

DAM systems support marketers in creating cohesive, multi-channel campaigns by providing easy access to the right assets for each channel. DAM helps marketers adapt content to fit the unique requirements of each platform, whether resizing images for social media or ensuring high-resolution assets are available for print.

A robust DAM system enables the "create once, publish everywhere" approach by storing assets in a way that makes them adaptable across formats and channels. This approach helps brands maintain a unified message and appearance, even while catering to the nuances of each platform.

Example: Multi-Channel Efficiency with DAM

For example, a marketing team launching a campaign across Instagram, LinkedIn, and their website can use the same set of assets, modified to fit each platform's specifications, directly from the DAM. This avoids duplicating work and helps ensure every channel carries a consistent visual and messaging theme.

Conclusion

A DAM system does more than organize assets; it empowers marketing teams to execute campaigns faster, ensures brand consistency, and supports collaborative, multi-channel marketing efforts. By adopting a DAM, organizations not only increase their operational efficiency but also position themselves to adapt more readily to an ever-evolving marketing landscape.

For marketers, a DAM is a strategic investment that transforms digital assets from static files into powerful tools that drive campaigns, elevate brand perception, and facilitate impactful storytelling. In the next chapter, we'll dive into building a business case for DAM and demonstrating its ROI to key stakeholders.

Chapter 2: Key Business Benefits of Implementing a DAM

Describing how DAM impacts operational efficiency, creative productivity, and overall marketing ROI

TL;DR

Implementing a DAM system delivers significant benefits for marketing teams, including improved efficiency, brand consistency, and speed to market. DAM centralizes assets, making it easy for teams to find and use approved content, which saves time and reduces redundant work. It also strengthens collaboration through streamlined workflows and approval processes, supporting faster, coordinated campaign execution. Additionally, DAM provides cost savings, valuable data insights, and enhanced compliance through controlled access and audit trails. Ultimately, a DAM system transforms digital assets into strategic tools, delivering measurable ROI and empowering marketers to focus on high-impact work.

Investing in a Digital Asset Management (DAM) system is more than just acquiring a new technology; it's a strategic decision that can drive measurable value across an organization. For marketers, the decision to implement a DAM comes down to its potential to improve efficiency, streamline processes, and provide tangible return on investment (ROI). This chapter dives into the key business benefits of DAM, from operational savings to enhanced brand consistency, and illustrates how a DAM can become a foundational asset for organizations looking to stay competitive in a content-driven marketplace.

Figure 2.1, Potential Benefits of Investments in Digital Asset Management (DAM)

2.1 Enhanced Efficiency and Productivity

DAM systems transform how teams store, search, and retrieve assets, which can significantly boost productivity. Marketers often waste hours searching for the right assets across scattered storage solutions, including cloud drives, email chains, or personal folders. DAM eliminates these inefficiencies by providing a centralized, searchable library of approved content.

- **Time Savings**: By reducing asset retrieval time, DAM allows marketers to allocate their time toward creative and strategic work rather than hunting for files.

- **Reduced Redundancies**: DAM minimizes duplicate work. With one source of truth, teams avoid re-creating assets that already exist, resulting in both time and cost savings.

Example: Efficiency in Action

A global cosmetics brand implemented a DAM system and reported a 35% reduction in time spent locating assets, freeing up significant resources for creative campaign work. This efficiency empowered their marketing team to deliver campaigns faster across multiple regions.

2.2 Improved Brand Consistency and Control

In today's multi-channel marketing environment, brand consistency is critical. Every digital asset—whether a logo, product image, or campaign banner—should reinforce the same message and visual identity. DAM helps enforce brand guidelines by storing only approved assets and making it easier to access consistent, on-brand content.

- **Centralized Control**: DAMs allow marketing and brand teams to manage assets centrally, reducing the risk of outdated or off-brand materials circulating.
- **Guidelines Enforcement**: Many DAMs include features to enforce branding rules, such as mandatory metadata fields, predefined templates, and watermarking, ensuring assets align with brand standards.

Example: Consistency with DAM

For example, a healthcare organization can store only compliant, approved assets in their DAM. When rolling out a national campaign, teams across regions can access approved assets without worrying about inconsistencies or compliance issues. This ensures every public-facing message remains on-brand and meets regulatory standards.

2.3 Accelerated Speed to Market

Marketing teams face constant pressure to launch campaigns quickly to stay ahead of competitors and respond to market changes. A DAM system's organizational structure enables marketers to access and deploy assets rapidly, accelerating campaign timelines.

- **Quick Asset Access**: With organized, easily searchable assets, teams can launch campaigns faster by having everything they need at their fingertips.
- **Multi-Channel Deployment**: Many DAMs integrate with content management systems (CMS) and social media platforms, allowing assets to be distributed directly from the DAM. This reduces friction and eliminates unnecessary steps in campaign execution.

Example: Speed to Market in Action

A sportswear brand leveraged its DAM to reduce the time it took to launch seasonal campaigns. By integrating their DAM with the CMS, they could push content live to their website and social channels instantly, reducing time to market by 25% and improving their responsiveness to trends.

2.4 Improved Collaboration and Workflow

A DAM enhances cross-functional collaboration by providing a common workspace where teams can access, edit, and approve assets in real-time. Creative, marketing, legal, and compliance teams can work together seamlessly, reducing bottlenecks and streamlining the asset review process.

- **Approval Workflows**: Many DAMs offer customizable workflows that allow teams to set up approval processes, ensuring assets are reviewed by the right stakeholders before going live.
- **Real-Time Collaboration**: DAMs allow users to comment, tag, and update assets in real-time, enabling feedback loops that shorten project timelines and reduce miscommunication.

Example: Collaborative Gains

A B2B technology company adopted a DAM with integrated approval workflows and saw collaboration between marketing and legal improve. By streamlining approvals and feedback within the DAM, they cut campaign lead times by 30%, allowing the marketing team to be more agile and responsive.

2.5 Cost Savings and ROI

While implementing a DAM is an investment, the potential cost savings are substantial, both in direct and indirect ways. By reducing redundant work, increasing productivity, and accelerating campaign timelines, a DAM quickly generates ROI.

- **Reduction in Redundant Asset Creation**: Without DAM, teams often recreate assets because they can't locate existing ones. DAM minimizes these redundancies, saving time and money.
- **Operational Efficiency**: DAM reduces the need for storage, minimizes asset duplication, and lowers the costs associated with inefficient workflows.
- **Measurable ROI**: DAM systems allow organizations to track usage metrics, such as time saved or campaign delivery speed, making it easy to quantify the financial impact.

Example: Quantifiable ROI

A consumer goods company calculated that their DAM saved them nearly $250,000 annually by eliminating duplicate asset creation and reducing time spent on asset management tasks. By monitoring these metrics, they were able to justify their investment and continue optimizing their asset management strategy.

2.6 Data-Driven Insights and Analytics

A DAM is not just a storage solution; it's a powerful data source that provides insights into asset performance and user engagement.

Marketers can track how often assets are used, in which campaigns, and by whom, enabling data-driven decisions on content effectiveness and ROI.

- **Asset Usage Tracking**: DAM analytics show which assets are popular or underutilized, helping teams refine their content strategy.
- **Performance Insights**: By linking DAM data with campaign metrics, marketers can gauge which types of assets drive engagement and conversion, allowing for a more strategic approach to content creation.

Example: Using Analytics to Improve Content

For instance, a fashion retailer uses its DAM analytics to monitor asset usage across campaigns. They noticed higher engagement with lifestyle imagery over product shots, prompting a shift in their visual content strategy to focus more on lifestyle images, leading to a 15% lift in engagement.

2.7 Enhanced Compliance and Risk Management

In industries like healthcare, finance, or retail, regulatory compliance is paramount. DAMs provide controlled access to assets, track usage, and offer digital rights management (DRM) features, ensuring compliance with legal and regulatory requirements.

- **Access Control**: DAM systems allow marketers to set permissions that control who can access, edit, or distribute assets.
- **Audit Trails**: Many DAMs maintain detailed logs of asset activity, providing an audit trail that can be essential for compliance purposes.
- **Rights Management**: By tracking licensing information and expiration dates, DAMs help prevent unauthorized usage, reducing legal risks.

Example: Compliance in Action

A pharmaceutical company leveraged DAM's DRM features to control usage rights and licensing information. By setting up permissions and automated alerts for expiring licenses, they minimized compliance risks and avoided fines related to unauthorized asset use.

Conclusion

A DAM system doesn't just simplify asset management; it's a strategic investment that drives efficiency, collaboration, brand consistency, and compliance. By providing easy access to on-brand assets and supporting faster, data-driven decision-making, DAM empowers marketers to focus on innovation and creativity. Whether reducing time-to-market, fostering collaboration, or saving on operational costs, DAM delivers measurable value that justifies its adoption.

In the next chapter, we'll dive into the key features and functionalities that define an effective DAM, including both core components and recent advancements in AI-powered capabilities. These insights will equip marketers with the knowledge to assess DAM systems based on their specific needs and maximize their benefits.

Chapter 3: Building a Strong Business Case for DAM Investment

Outlining steps to present a convincing case to stakeholders, including key metrics and KPIs that demonstrate the value of DAM.

TL;DR

Building a strong business case for a DAM system involves demonstrating its impact on productivity, brand consistency, compliance, and ROI. Key steps include identifying the unique needs of stakeholders (marketing, IT, legal, finance), outlining specific business problems DAM addresses, and quantifying benefits like time savings and reduced redundant

asset creation. Highlight potential ROI by estimating cost savings in content production, storage, and operational efficiency. Address objections (e.g., cost, complexity) with solutions like phased implementation and training. Finally, align the case with strategic goals, such as digital transformation and competitive advantage, to gain leadership buy-in.

Investing in a Digital Asset Management (DAM) system is a strategic decision that often requires buy-in from leadership, budget approval, and clear evidence of ROI. For marketers, building a compelling business case for DAM involves demonstrating how it directly benefits the organization, from operational efficiency to increased brand consistency and compliance. In this chapter, we'll outline how to construct a persuasive business case for DAM, highlighting the key areas of impact, the metrics to measure success, and the ways to communicate DAM's strategic value to stakeholders.

3.1 Identifying Key Stakeholders and Their Needs

Building a successful business case starts with understanding the perspectives of key stakeholders across the organization. Different teams will have unique needs and expectations from a DAM, and addressing these in your proposal can increase support and collaboration.

- **Marketing and Creative Teams**: These teams need quick, reliable access to assets for content creation, campaign execution, and brand consistency.
- **IT and Security Teams**: IT stakeholders are concerned with integration, security, and infrastructure, ensuring the DAM aligns with the organization's tech stack and compliance requirements.
- **Legal and Compliance Teams**: For industries with strict regulatory standards, legal teams value a DAM's ability to track licensing, usage, and compliance with brand guidelines.
- **Finance and Leadership**: Financial decision-makers focus on ROI, operational efficiency, and cost savings. They want to see how a DAM can impact the bottom line and provide long-term value.

Example: Understanding Stakeholder Needs

In a large retail organization, the marketing team wants a DAM for faster campaign rollouts, while the finance team requires a clear outline of cost savings and ROI. Tailoring the business case to each team's priorities can strengthen alignment and expedite the approval process.

3.2 Defining the Core Business Problems that DAM Solves

A powerful business case starts by clearly articulating the specific problems a DAM will solve. By aligning these pain points with organizational goals, you can emphasize the practical value of a DAM.

- **Inefficient Asset Management**: Describe how scattered or redundant storage locations make it difficult to locate assets, causing delays and reduced productivity.
- **Inconsistent Brand Representation**: Explain the risks of using outdated or off-brand assets, which can erode brand reputation and customer trust.
- **Limited Collaboration**: Show how DAM can improve cross-functional collaboration by providing a centralized platform for asset sharing, editing, and approval.
- **Compliance Risks**: Outline how a DAM can mitigate risks related to licensing, regulatory compliance, and usage rights by centralizing and controlling access to assets.

Example: Articulating Business Challenges

A healthcare organization may face strict compliance requirements for marketing assets, including privacy laws and licensing limitations. A DAM solution addresses these issues by storing assets securely, managing permissions, and tracking usage rights, reducing compliance risks significantly.

3.3 Quantifying the Benefits of DAM with Metrics and KPIs

To build a compelling case for DAM, it's essential to translate its benefits into quantifiable metrics that demonstrate ROI. Here are some KPIs that can strengthen your business case:

- **Time Saved in Asset Retrieval**: Calculate the average time employees spend searching for assets without a DAM and how much time could be saved with a centralized system.
- **Reduction in Redundant Asset Creation**: Quantify the costs associated with duplicate asset creation and demonstrate how DAM minimizes these expenses.
- **Improvement in Campaign Speed**: Highlight the potential for faster campaign rollouts, showing how DAM reduces time-to-market and enables timely responses to market trends.
- **Increased Asset Utilization**: Track the frequency of asset usage to demonstrate that a DAM encourages asset reuse, maximizing the value of each asset created.

Example: Metrics That Prove Value

A tech company calculated that their marketing team saved 20 hours per month on asset searches after implementing DAM. By quantifying this efficiency gain, they demonstrated a tangible return on investment to leadership.

3.4 Estimating Potential ROI and Cost Savings

ROI is a critical factor for decision-makers when evaluating DAM investments. Calculating potential cost savings and productivity gains can solidify the financial case for DAM. Below are some areas to consider when estimating ROI:

- **Reduced Costs of Storage**: By centralizing assets, DAM can reduce or even eliminate costs associated with redundant storage solutions.
- **Lower Content Creation Costs**: DAM encourages the reuse of existing assets, saving costs that would otherwise go toward creating similar content.
- **Operational Savings**: Reduced time spent on searching for assets, managing permissions, and coordinating across teams leads to significant operational savings.
- **Improved Campaign Performance**: DAM enhances brand consistency and speed-to-market, which can positively impact campaign results and revenue generation.

Example: Calculating ROI for a DAM

A financial services company analyzed the cost of duplicating assets across different departments and calculated that DAM would save $50,000 annually in storage and content creation costs. These savings were a key point in gaining leadership approval for DAM investment.

3.5 Addressing Potential Challenges and Objections

Understanding and proactively addressing potential objections can strengthen your business case. Common objections to DAM include concerns about cost, implementation complexity, and user adoption.

- **Objection: High Initial Cost**
  Response: Highlight the potential for long-term ROI through cost savings, efficiency gains, and improved asset reuse.
- **Objection: Complexity of Implementation**
  Response: Outline an implementation plan that includes training, onboarding, and ongoing support to ensure a smooth transition.
- **Objection: Low User Adoption**
  Response: Emphasize the benefits of a user-friendly interface and provide case studies showing high adoption rates in similar organizations.

Example: Handling Objections

A global CPG company anticipated concerns about adoption among creative teams. They proposed an initial pilot program with targeted training sessions to demonstrate the ease and value of the DAM system, gaining support from potential users.

3.6 Developing a Step-by-Step Implementation Roadmap

A well-structured roadmap can reassure stakeholders that the DAM implementation will be smooth and efficient. Outline the key phases of the DAM project, including timelines, milestones, and any necessary resources.

- **Phase 1: Needs Assessment and Vendor Selection**
  Conduct needs analysis and gather requirements from each team. Evaluate potential vendors based on their ability to meet these requirements.
- **Phase 2: DAM Configuration and Setup**
  Customize the DAM system to align with your organization's taxonomy, metadata standards, and folder structures.
- **Phase 3: Training and Onboarding**
  Develop a training plan that includes hands-on workshops, user guides, and a support framework.
- **Phase 4: Launch and Feedback**
  Roll out the DAM to all users and gather feedback to identify any areas for optimization.

Example: Implementation Roadmap

A retail brand created a six-month implementation roadmap for their DAM, starting with stakeholder workshops, moving to configuration, and ending with a phased rollout to ensure a seamless transition for all teams.

3.7 Communicating the Strategic Value of DAM to Leadership

When presenting your business case, it's important to focus on how DAM aligns with the organization's broader strategic goals.

Emphasize how DAM supports long-term objectives, such as digital transformation, customer experience, and competitive agility.

- **Support for Digital Transformation**: Explain how DAM acts as a foundation for digital initiatives, providing a scalable solution that grows with the organization.
- **Enhanced Customer Experience**: By enabling fast, consistent, and personalized content delivery, DAM can improve customer engagement and loyalty.
- **Competitive Advantage**: Highlight how DAM increases marketing agility, helping your organization stay ahead in a rapidly changing market.

Example: Strategic Value Presentation

A B2B SaaS company aligned their DAM proposal with their digital transformation goals, showing how DAM would enable faster content delivery and improve customer experience. This alignment with strategic initiatives secured leadership support and accelerated approval.

Conclusion

A well-prepared business case not only highlights the operational and financial benefits of a DAM system but also demonstrates its alignment with strategic goals. By quantifying key metrics, anticipating objections, and developing an actionable implementation roadmap, marketers can create a persuasive argument that resonates with all stakeholders. With a DAM, organizations not only streamline their asset management but also gain a competitive edge in today's content-driven world.

In the next chapter, we'll discuss the core features and functionalities that marketers should look for in a DAM system, including essential components and AI-enhanced capabilities that add value and adaptability to the platform.

Part 2:
Core and Advanced Features of a DAM

Choosing the right Digital Asset Management (DAM) system requires a deep understanding of the essential and advanced features that support both day-to-day marketing operations and long-term brand strategy. In Part 2, we'll examine the critical functionalities that define a high-performing DAM, including both core features and innovative enhancements like AI-driven tagging and intelligent search. While core features form the backbone of an effective DAM system, advanced functionalities can offer marketers a competitive edge, helping them work faster, collaborate seamlessly, and make data-informed decisions.

The Agile Brand Guide: Digital Asset Management | 43

This part of the book is structured to guide you through the specific attributes that matter most for marketers. We'll start by covering core components like metadata, search, version control, and permissions—features that ensure efficient asset organization, retrieval, and access control. Next, we'll explore advanced capabilities such as AI, automated workflows, and integrations with other tools in the marketing stack, which can elevate your DAM from a basic repository to a strategic asset.

Understanding these features not only helps you assess DAM platforms but also prepares you to maximize the value of your chosen system. By aligning DAM functionalities with your organization's unique goals, you can build a robust asset management system that drives consistency, efficiency, and creative potential across your marketing initiatives.

Chapter 4:
Core Features Every DAM Should Have

Exploring fundamental features: metadata tagging, search functionality, version control, access controls, and permissions.

TL;DR

A strong DAM system includes core features that streamline asset organization, retrieval, and collaboration. Key features include metadata and tagging for quick searchability, robust search and filtering options, and version control to manage asset revisions. Access control and permissions protect sensitive content, while collaboration tools support efficient

feedback and approvals. Download options enable users to access assets in multiple formats, and analytics provide insights into asset usage, helping teams make data-driven decisions. Together, these core features empower marketers to manage and leverage digital assets effectively, ensuring consistent brand representation and operational efficiency.

Choosing the right Digital Asset Management (DAM) system starts with understanding the core features that make a DAM truly effective. A robust DAM platform provides more than basic storage; it offers essential tools to organize, retrieve, and control assets while enabling collaboration across teams. In this chapter, we'll break down the key features every DAM should include, from metadata and search capabilities to version control and permissions. By understanding these foundational elements, marketers can make informed decisions when evaluating potential DAM systems and ensure that the chosen solution meets their team's everyday needs.

4.1 Metadata and Tagging

Metadata is one of the most critical elements of any DAM system. It's the descriptive data about an asset—such as keywords, author, usage rights, and creation date—that makes assets searchable and organized. Effective metadata and tagging structures allow marketers to retrieve assets quickly, even from large, complex libraries.

- **Automatic Metadata Tagging**: Some DAM systems offer AI-powered automatic tagging, which assigns metadata to new assets as they're uploaded. This feature reduces the manual workload and helps keep metadata consistent.
- **Customizable Metadata Fields**: Look for a DAM that allows customization of metadata fields to fit your organization's unique needs. Custom fields can reflect industry-specific information, such as campaign season, product type, or geographic region.

Example: Metadata for Efficient Search

A global beverage company uses custom metadata fields for "product type," "region," and "season" to organize its assets. When marketers need to launch a summer campaign in Europe, they can easily filter for relevant assets, saving significant time in asset retrieval.

4.2 Search and Filtering Capabilities

Search functionality is the backbone of any DAM system. A DAM should allow users to locate assets quickly and accurately, even if they only remember partial information about the asset. Advanced search and filtering features make this possible by leveraging metadata, keywords, and other identifying information.

- **Keyword Search**: A standard feature in DAM systems, keyword search enables users to type in relevant terms to find assets tagged with those words.

- **Faceted Search and Filters**: Faceted search allows users to narrow down results by applying multiple filters, such as asset type, date created, or campaign name. This layered search capability can dramatically speed up the asset discovery process.

Example: Accelerated Search for Campaign Assets

A fashion retailer relies on faceted search to quickly locate assets by season, style, and color. This capability allows their marketing team to retrieve assets within seconds, significantly improving the speed of campaign planning and execution.

4.3 Version Control

Version control is essential for managing updates, revisions, and different iterations of an asset. With version control, users can track changes, revert to previous versions if needed, and ensure that only the latest, approved versions of assets are available for use.

- **Automatic Versioning**: Many DAMs automatically save new versions when changes are made, making it easy to review the history of an asset and maintain a comprehensive record.
- **Rollback Capability**: The ability to revert to previous versions helps prevent issues that arise from unintended edits or changes, ensuring that the brand maintains control over asset quality.

Example: Managing Asset Versions

An advertising agency uses version control to manage iterations of client assets. By keeping each revision linked within the DAM, team members can quickly access the latest approved version and avoid using outdated content, which can be especially important when working with regulated brands.

4.4 Access Control and Permissions

A DAM is only as effective as its ability to control access and permissions. Different users across an organization will need varying levels of access to assets, depending on their roles. Effective access control protects sensitive content, ensures compliance, and enables only approved team members to make edits or share assets externally.

- **Role-Based Access Control (RBAC)**: RBAC allows DAM administrators to assign access based on a user's role, ensuring each user sees only what they need to.
- **Permission Levels**: Look for DAMs with customizable permission levels, such as view-only, edit, and approval rights, which are essential for managing content securely and reducing the risk of unauthorized edits.

Example: Ensuring Secure Access

A healthcare organization with strict compliance requirements uses role-based access in their DAM, ensuring that only authorized personnel can access patient-related content. This setup prevents unauthorized access and supports regulatory compliance.

4.5 Collaboration Tools

Effective collaboration is critical in marketing and creative teams, where assets often require input and approvals from multiple stakeholders. Collaboration tools within a DAM streamline workflows by allowing users to comment, provide feedback, and assign tasks directly within the platform.

- **Commenting and Annotations**: Many DAMs support commenting directly on assets, which is useful for creative teams needing feedback on drafts or revisions.
- **Approval Workflows**: Approval workflows allow users to request feedback and approvals from stakeholders, ensuring assets go through the right review stages before publication.

Example: Streamlined Creative Collaboration

A consumer electronics brand uses approval workflows to streamline collaboration between its creative and marketing teams. Designers upload assets to the DAM, tag relevant stakeholders, and receive approval directly within the platform, reducing the need for email-based communication and shortening review cycles.

4.6 Download and Format Options

Marketing assets often need to be resized or reformatted to fit specific channels, from social media to print. A DAM that supports multiple download options, including predefined formats, ensures that marketers can quickly access assets in the format they need without relying on a designer to make adjustments.

- **Preset Download Options**: Some DAMs allow users to download assets in predefined sizes and formats, such as resizing an image for social media or converting it to a lower-resolution file.
- **On-the-Fly Conversion**: Advanced DAM systems offer on-the-fly conversion, enabling users to download assets in various formats directly from the DAM, which can save time and increase productivity.

Example: Multi-Format Asset Access

A B2B SaaS company uses its DAM's format options to adapt a single asset for various channels. They can download a high-resolution file for print or a web-optimized version for digital campaigns, eliminating delays and ensuring content is fit-for-purpose.

4.7 Analytics and Reporting

A DAM with built-in analytics can provide valuable insights into how assets are being used, helping marketing teams make data-driven decisions on content creation and optimization. By tracking metrics such as asset views, downloads, and usage frequency, teams can gauge which types of content are most valuable and adjust their strategies accordingly.

- **Usage Reports**: Usage reports track how frequently assets are accessed, shared, or downloaded, helping to identify popular content and guiding future asset creation.
- **User Activity Monitoring**: User activity data can help administrators understand how employees interact with the DAM, identify potential training needs, and improve user experience.

Example: Data-Driven Content Strategy

A non-profit organization uses DAM analytics to understand which assets resonate most with their audience. By tracking downloads and views, they can focus their content strategy on producing similar high-performing assets, driving engagement and improving campaign outcomes.

4.8 Asset Expiration and Archiving

A DAM should include features for asset expiration and archiving, particularly useful for organizations with content that becomes outdated or requires periodic reviews. Expiration and archiving ensure that only relevant, up-to-date assets are accessible, reducing the risk of outdated content being used.

- **Automated Expiration Dates**: Some DAMs allow users to set expiration dates for assets, automatically moving them to an archive once the date is reached.

- **Archiving Rules**: Customized archiving rules help keep the DAM organized, ensuring outdated content doesn't clutter the active asset library.

Example: Managing Seasonal Content

A retail brand uses asset expiration dates to manage seasonal assets, automatically archiving holiday campaign content once it's no longer relevant. This keeps the DAM uncluttered and ensures only current assets are accessible to teams.

Conclusion

Core features like metadata, search, version control, access permissions, and collaboration tools form the backbone of a powerful DAM system. Together, these features allow marketers to organize, control, and collaborate on assets seamlessly. A DAM that includes robust search, user-friendly permissions, and detailed reporting not only streamlines day-to-day tasks but also ensures long-term brand consistency, compliance, and operational efficiency.

In the next chapter, we'll explore advanced features that go beyond these core functionalities, including AI-powered capabilities and customizable integrations that add even more value to your DAM system.

Chapter 5: Advanced Features That Set a DAM Apart

Exploring "nice-to-have" features: integrations with other marketing tools, collaborative tools, and custom workflows.

TL;DR

Advanced features transform a DAM from basic storage to a powerful strategic tool. Key advanced capabilities include AI-driven tagging and image recognition, customizable workflow automation, and integration with other marketing tools, which boost productivity and streamline processes. Other valuable features include rights management for tracking

licenses, enhanced security with DRM and watermarking, automated archiving for content lifecycle management, and in-depth analytics for data-driven insights. By leveraging these advanced functionalities, marketers can optimize asset management, improve collaboration, and create more effective, consistent campaigns across all channels.

While core features form the foundation of any Digital Asset Management (DAM) system, advanced features add significant value by enhancing productivity, personalizing user experiences, and adapting to the evolving needs of modern marketing teams. As DAM technology advances, new capabilities powered by artificial intelligence (AI) and integration options have emerged, setting leading DAM platforms apart from the basics. This chapter explores advanced features that can transform a DAM from a simple asset repository to a strategic marketing tool. By understanding these options, marketers can identify the additional functionalities that provide the greatest value for their teams.

5.1 AI-Powered Tagging and Recognition

Artificial intelligence has brought new efficiency to DAM through automated tagging and image recognition, which can save time, reduce manual work, and improve search accuracy. With AI-powered tagging, DAM systems can automatically apply relevant metadata to new assets as they are uploaded, making it easier for users to find what they need.

- **Automatic Tagging**: AI algorithms analyze an asset's content and apply relevant keywords, colors, people, locations, and objects as tags, which improves asset organization without requiring manual input.
- **Image and Facial Recognition**: AI-powered recognition technology identifies people and objects in images, tagging them accordingly. This feature is particularly useful for organizations that manage large volumes of images with recurring subjects or themes.

Example: AI Tagging for Streamlined Search

A media company leverages AI tagging to automatically label uploaded images with keywords based on content. This saves their creative team hours of manual tagging and enhances search accuracy, as assets are tagged consistently and contextually from the start.

5.2 Customizable Workflow Automation

While sometimes this can fall into the category of Content Management Platforms (CMPs), some advanced DAMs offer workflow automation tools that support custom processes, allowing marketing teams to automate repetitive tasks and optimize the flow of assets from creation to approval. Customizable workflows enable users to create tailored processes for asset review, feedback, and approval stages, ensuring assets go through the right checkpoints.

- **Approval and Review Workflows**: Automated workflows guide assets through predefined steps, such as creative review, legal approval, and final publishing. Notifications alert stakeholders to review or approve assets, keeping projects on track.
- **Task Assignment and Tracking**: Some DAMs allow users to assign specific tasks, such as editing or tagging, directly within the system. This keeps teams aligned and reduces the need for external communication, like emails, to move assets through the pipeline.

Example: Custom Workflow for Campaign Approvals

A global consumer goods company uses customizable workflows in their DAM to streamline campaign approvals. Assets move through an automated approval pipeline, notifying regional marketing managers to approve or revise content before it is launched in each market. This structure ensures consistent quality and brand alignment across global teams.

5.3 Integration with Marketing Technology Stack

Modern DAM systems integrate seamlessly with other marketing tools, enhancing the utility of DAM and ensuring that assets are accessible across the marketing ecosystem. Integrations with content management systems (CMS), customer relationship management (CRM) platforms, social media schedulers, and project management tools allow assets to flow smoothly from one platform to another.

- **CMS Integration**: Integrating a DAM with a CMS allows marketers to access assets directly within their web content management platform, simplifying website content updates.
- **CRM and Personalization Tools**: DAM integrations with CRM and personalization tools enable marketers to deliver targeted, personalized content to specific audience segments, using data to drive content choices.
- **Social Media Scheduling**: DAMs that integrate with social media tools allow users to access, select, and schedule assets for social channels directly from the DAM, saving time and maintaining brand consistency.

Example: Seamless Asset Use Across Channels

An e-commerce company integrates its DAM with its CMS and social media scheduling tool, allowing the team to pull assets directly from the DAM for website updates and social posts. This integration eliminates the need to download and re-upload assets, streamlining the publishing process and ensuring consistency.

5.4 AI-Driven Content Recommendations

Some advanced DAMs provide AI-driven content recommendations that suggest relevant assets based on the user's needs, project requirements, or historical usage data. These recommendations can increase productivity by surfacing assets that might otherwise be overlooked and help teams maintain brand consistency.

- **Content Similarity Matching**: AI-powered similarity matching recommends assets similar to the one being viewed, enabling marketers to find visually aligned or thematically consistent content.
- **Usage-Based Recommendations**: Based on historical data, the DAM suggests assets that were popular in similar campaigns, helping marketers quickly find high-performing content that aligns with their goals.

Example: Boosting Campaign Efficiency with Recommendations

A retail brand uses an AI-driven DAM to suggest assets for upcoming campaigns based on past successful assets. By recommending images and graphics that performed well in similar campaigns, the DAM speeds up the content selection process and improves campaign effectiveness.

5.5 Rights Management and License Tracking

For organizations managing multiple licensed assets, DAMs with advanced rights management capabilities can help track usage rights and licenses. Rights management tools ensure that assets are used within approved timeframes, geographic locations, and channels, reducing legal risks associated with unauthorized use.

- **License Expiration Alerts**: DAMs can alert users when an asset's license is nearing expiration, helping teams stay compliant and preventing unlicensed usage.
- **Usage Restrictions**: Some DAMs allow users to set restrictions, such as limiting the use of assets to specific regions or campaigns, which prevents accidental misuse.

Example: Staying Compliant with License Tracking

A media company that regularly licenses content from third-party photographers uses DAM rights management to track license expirations and usage restrictions. The DAM alerts them when licenses are about to expire, allowing them to renew or replace assets before a campaign goes live, ensuring legal compliance.

5.6 Enhanced Security Features

Advanced security is essential for organizations handling sensitive or high-value assets. Some DAM systems offer features like digital rights management (DRM), watermarking, and advanced encryption, ensuring that assets remain secure and protected from unauthorized access.

- **Digital Rights Management (DRM)**: DRM restricts how assets can be used, copied, or shared, providing an additional layer of control and security.

- **Watermarking**: Watermarking protects proprietary or sensitive images by adding a visible mark (like a logo) to prevent unauthorized usage.
- **User Authentication and Permissions**: Enhanced security DAMs may include multi-factor authentication and granular permission settings to control access at a detailed level.

Example: Protecting Sensitive Assets

A financial services firm uses DRM and watermarking within its DAM to secure confidential presentations and research reports. Only authorized personnel have access, and watermarks discourage unauthorized distribution, keeping sensitive assets safe.

5.7 Digital Asset Expiry and Archiving Automation

Asset expiration and archiving automation keep the DAM organized and up-to-date by automatically archiving outdated content or removing assets that are no longer relevant. This feature is especially useful for organizations with seasonal campaigns or time-sensitive content.

- **Automated Archiving**: Assets can be automatically moved to an archive based on expiration dates, reducing clutter and ensuring only relevant content is available.

- **Scheduled Deletion**: For assets that need to be removed permanently, some DAMs offer scheduled deletion features, ensuring obsolete content is securely removed after a set period.

Example: Managing Seasonal Content Lifecycle

A sports brand manages a vast collection of seasonal assets for its spring, summer, and winter lines. With automated archiving, the DAM moves assets to an archive after each season ends, keeping the asset library current and uncluttered.

5.8 Data Analytics and Insights

While basic DAMs provide some usage reporting, advanced DAM systems offer deeper analytics to inform marketing strategies. By tracking asset performance, user behavior, and usage trends, DAM analytics can reveal valuable insights that help marketing teams optimize their content strategies.

- **Asset Performance Tracking**: This feature shows how often assets are viewed, downloaded, or used in campaigns, identifying high-performing content and areas for improvement.
- **User Engagement Analysis**: By analyzing how different teams use the DAM, marketers can identify potential training needs or adjust the DAM's configuration to better suit users' needs.

- **Campaign Attribution**: Some DAMs link assets to campaign metrics, providing insights into how certain assets impact engagement and conversion rates.

Example: Data-Driven Campaign Optimization

A B2B company uses DAM analytics to track the effectiveness of their white papers and infographics. By identifying which assets generate the most downloads and engagement, they focus on creating similar content, leading to improved campaign performance and resource allocation.

Conclusion

Advanced features like AI-driven tagging, workflow automation, and enhanced integrations distinguish high-performing DAM systems, transforming them into strategic tools for today's marketers. These capabilities help organizations automate repetitive tasks, provide data-driven insights, and deliver content quickly across multiple channels. By understanding and leveraging these advanced features, marketers can elevate the utility of their DAM and gain a significant advantage in an increasingly content-driven market.

In the next chapter, we'll explore how to evaluate and select a DAM, focusing on identifying the right teams to involve, aligning requirements with business goals, and assessing different vendors based on both core and advanced functionalities.

Chapter 6:
Leveraging AI in DAM Systems

Discussing AI-driven features like automatic tagging, facial recognition, smart cropping, and content recommendations and the benefits of AI-powered asset categorization, metadata enhancement, and search capabilities.

TL;DR

AI-powered features in DAM systems unlock new efficiencies and insights for marketing teams. Automated tagging and intelligent search improve asset discoverability, while facial recognition and sentiment analysis help categorize and select visuals that align with campaign goals. AI-driven content recommendations and predictive analytics offer data-driven *suggestions, enabling marketers to use high-performing assets and anticipate content needs. Dynamic personalization tailors visuals for specific audiences across channels, enhancing engagement. By leveraging these AI capabilities, marketers can streamline workflows, enhance personalization, and create more impactful, data-informed content strategies.*

Artificial intelligence (AI) is rapidly transforming the functionality and value of Digital Asset Management (DAM) systems, offering unprecedented automation, personalization, and insight. By integrating AI into DAM, marketers can streamline processes, improve asset discoverability, and extract actionable insights from their content. As AI becomes increasingly sophisticated, its applications in DAM continue to expand—from auto-tagging and smart search to predictive analytics and content recommendations. This chapter explores the various AI-driven features that can enhance a DAM's capabilities and help marketing teams maximize efficiency and creativity.

6.1 Automated Metadata Tagging

AI-driven metadata tagging is one of the most impactful applications of AI in DAM. Traditionally, tagging assets with metadata is a manual, time-consuming task, prone to inconsistencies that can affect searchability. AI automates this process by analyzing the content of assets—identifying objects, colors, scenes, and even emotions in images or videos—and applying relevant tags. This capability saves time and ensures consistency across the entire asset library.

- **Visual Recognition for Images**: AI can detect elements like people, places, colors, and objects within images, tagging them automatically. For example, a photo with a beach setting might be tagged with "beach," "outdoors," and "water."
- **Text Recognition (OCR)**: Optical character recognition (OCR) identifies and extracts text from images, making assets with embedded text, such as infographics or presentations, easily searchable by their content.

Example: Streamlined Tagging with AI

A travel agency using a DAM with AI tagging can upload a new set of vacation images, which the system automatically tags with keywords like "mountain," "beach," "sunset," or "hiking." This automated process reduces the time spent on tagging and increases search efficiency, allowing marketers to quickly locate images for different campaigns.

6.2 Intelligent Search and Discovery

AI enhances search functionality in DAM by interpreting search queries and delivering more relevant results. Unlike traditional search, which relies solely on keywords, AI-driven search can understand context, synonyms, and visual similarities, making it easier for users to find the assets they need, even if they don't know the exact keywords.

- **Natural Language Processing (NLP)**: NLP allows the DAM to interpret conversational search queries, such as "beach photos with sunset," improving search accuracy and user experience.
- **Visual Similarity Search**: This feature enables users to find assets that visually resemble a selected image, which is helpful for finding similar visuals across campaigns or discovering assets with consistent themes.

Example: Improved Search Accuracy with NLP

A fashion brand using an AI-enabled DAM can search for "summer dresses with beach backgrounds," and the system will recognize contextually relevant assets. By understanding the intent behind the query, the DAM delivers more accurate results, enabling the brand to create visually cohesive campaigns.

6.3 Facial Recognition and Asset Categorization

Facial recognition is a powerful AI tool within DAM, especially for companies that manage large volumes of image or video assets featuring people. Facial recognition software identifies individuals across assets, applying tags with their names or roles, which can be invaluable for organizing content in industries like media, sports, or retail.

- **Tagging People and Roles**: Facial recognition tags individuals by name, role, or other identifiers, helping users quickly locate assets featuring specific people.

- **Categorizing by Identity**: DAMs can automatically group assets based on recognized faces, allowing users to search for images of a particular spokesperson, model, or executive without manual tagging.

Example: Facial Recognition for Efficient Categorization

A sports franchise uses facial recognition in its DAM to tag and categorize images of players, coaches, and other team members. This feature allows the marketing team to easily pull assets featuring specific players, enhancing their social media and merchandising efforts.

6.4 Content Recommendations Based on AI Insights

AI-driven content recommendations use machine learning to suggest assets based on patterns, user behavior, and past campaign performance. By analyzing historical data, the DAM can identify assets that align with a user's current project or recommend high-performing visuals from previous campaigns, helping marketers create more impactful, data-backed content.

- **Similarity-Based Recommendations**: AI suggests assets similar to the ones a user frequently accesses, allowing for cohesive content choices.

- **Performance-Based Suggestions**: AI analyzes which assets performed well in past campaigns and recommends them for future projects, increasing the likelihood of using high-impact visuals.

Example: Data-Driven Recommendations for Campaigns

An e-commerce company uses AI-driven content recommendations to suggest visuals based on successful past campaigns. By recommending similar product images and themes, the DAM helps the marketing team quickly locate high-performing assets, reducing campaign preparation time and enhancing content effectiveness.

6.5 Predictive Analytics for Asset Usage and Strategy

AI can provide predictive analytics in DAM systems, offering insights into asset performance and potential future trends. Predictive analytics can help marketers understand which assets are likely to resonate with audiences based on historical performance, seasonal trends, or industry shifts, allowing them to make proactive content decisions.

- **Forecasting Content Demand**: AI analyzes historical usage patterns to predict which assets will be in demand, helping marketers prepare relevant content in advance.
- **Audience Preferences and Trends**: Predictive models can highlight trends in audience engagement, showing which types of assets are likely to drive future interactions and conversions.

Example: Leveraging Predictive Analytics for Seasonal Campaigns

A retailer uses predictive analytics in their DAM to anticipate the types of visuals that perform best during holiday seasons, such as product images or lifestyle photos. This insight enables the marketing team to prioritize relevant assets and prepare content that aligns with anticipated audience preferences.

6.6 Sentiment Analysis for Video and Image Assets

Some advanced DAMs include sentiment analysis, which evaluates the tone or emotional content of video and image assets. By understanding the sentiment behind visuals, marketers can select content that aligns with specific campaign goals, whether they're aiming to evoke excitement, warmth, or trust.

- **Emotion Detection**: AI recognizes emotions in people's expressions in images and videos, tagging assets with keywords like "happy," "excited," or "calm," which aids in selecting visuals for targeted emotional impact.
- **Tone Matching**: Sentiment analysis allows marketers to search for assets with specific tones, ensuring cohesive messaging and emotional resonance across all campaign materials.

Example: Sentiment-Driven Campaigns

An environmental non-profit organization uses sentiment analysis to select visuals that evoke trust and empathy for their campaigns. By focusing on images with a calm and hopeful tone, they enhance the emotional impact of their messaging, creating a more effective and resonant campaign.

6.7 Dynamic Personalization for Multi-Channel Marketing

AI-enabled DAMs can support dynamic content personalization, automatically selecting assets based on specific audience characteristics or behaviors. This feature allows marketers to deliver personalized experiences across channels, such as websites, email, or social media, without needing to manually select different visuals for each audience segment.

- **Audience-Based Recommendations**: AI recommends assets for different customer segments, such as high-value customers or first-time visitors, tailoring the content experience to each audience.
- **Automated Asset Adaptation**: Some DAMs enable on-the-fly adjustments to assets, such as resizing or reformatting, based on the platform and audience type, which ensures that assets are optimized across all channels.

Example: Automated Personalization for Email Campaigns

A travel brand uses their DAM's dynamic personalization feature to tailor email visuals for different customer segments. High-frequency travelers receive exotic destination images, while first-time customers see popular local getaways. This personalization boosts engagement by aligning content with each customer's interests.

Conclusion

AI capabilities in DAM offer far more than simple automation—they enable intelligent, data-driven asset management that supports marketers in delivering faster, more impactful, and personalized content. With AI-driven features like automated tagging, intelligent search, facial recognition, content recommendations, predictive analytics, sentiment analysis, and dynamic personalization, marketers can streamline workflows, enhance asset discoverability, and align visuals with campaign goals and audience preferences. Leveraging AI in DAM not only boosts efficiency but also empowers marketers to create content that resonates deeply with their audiences.

In the next chapter, we'll delve into the process of evaluating a DAM, discussing the teams involved, defining requirements, and assessing vendors to ensure that both core and advanced features align with your organization's goals.

Part 3: Evaluating and Choosing the Right DAM

With a well-planned selection and evaluation process complete, the next stage in the journey is bringing your Digital Asset Management (DAM) system to life within your organization. Implementation is a critical phase that goes beyond technical setup—it's about laying the foundation for a DAM that will drive productivity, support collaboration, and deliver strategic value. Part 3 provides a roadmap for successful DAM implementation, from creating a detailed project plan to configuring metadata, establishing workflows, and training users.

This part of the book is designed to help you not only launch your DAM effectively but also set up practices that ensure long-term success. A well-implemented DAM should evolve with your organization, adapting to new demands and scaling as your asset library grows. We'll explore how to promote user adoption, monitor performance, and gather feedback, creating a culture of continuous improvement. By following these best practices, your organization can fully leverage the DAM's capabilities, making it an invaluable tool for efficiency, brand consistency, and collaboration.

Ultimately, the implementation phase is about building a system that meets your organization's needs today while setting the stage for sustainable, adaptable growth.

Chapter 7: Identifying Stakeholders and Assembling a Team for Evaluation

Exploring roles within the marketing team and beyond, including IT, legal, creative, and content teams and how to conduct requirements gathering from each department.

TL;DR

Selecting a DAM requires input from multiple departments to ensure it meets organization-wide needs. Key stakeholders include marketing, creative, IT, legal, and finance, each bringing unique priorities: marketing values search and *integration, creative needs version control and workflows, IT focuses on security and compatibility, legal requires rights management, and finance evaluates ROI. Building a cross-functional evaluation team helps address all these perspectives, fostering collaboration and alignment. By working together, these stakeholders can choose a DAM that enhances efficiency, compliance, and long-term value, ensuring it supports both daily operations and strategic goals.*

Selecting a Digital Asset Management (DAM) system is a significant decision that impacts multiple departments across an organization. Because DAM will serve as a centralized hub for organizing, storing, and distributing digital assets, it's essential to involve the right stakeholders in the evaluation process. Engaging a diverse team ensures the DAM system meets the needs of various departments, from marketing and creative to IT and legal, aligning with organizational goals and promoting cross-functional support. In this chapter, we'll identify the key stakeholders to involve, discuss their unique perspectives, and outline how to build a collaborative team that will make informed, strategic decisions about your DAM investment.

7.1 Key Stakeholders to Include in the DAM Evaluation Process

To make a successful DAM selection, it's critical to gather input from a range of departments. Each group brings its own requirements and priorities to the table, and involving them early can help ensure the DAM meets the broader needs of the organization. Here are the primary stakeholders to consider:

- **Marketing Team**: As primary DAM users, marketers need quick, reliable access to assets for campaigns, social media, email marketing, and personalization. Their priorities include intuitive search functionality, metadata options, and integrations with other marketing tools like CMS and CRM.
- **Creative Team**: This team is responsible for creating and managing visual assets, such as images, videos, and graphics. Creatives require DAM features that support version control, easy collaboration, and automated workflows for review and approval. They also benefit from AI-powered features like automated tagging, which streamline asset organization.
- **IT Department**: The IT team ensures the DAM aligns with the organization's technical requirements, including compatibility with the tech stack, security, and data management standards. They play a crucial role in evaluating the DAM's scalability, integration capabilities, and overall infrastructure requirements.
- **Legal and Compliance**: In industries with strict regulatory requirements, the legal team ensures that the DAM meets compliance standards, particularly around content rights, usage restrictions, and licensing. They prioritize features like rights

management, permissions, and audit trails to maintain regulatory compliance and mitigate risk.
- **Finance Team**: The finance department evaluates DAM investment from a cost and ROI perspective. Their focus is on the financial viability of the DAM, weighing the upfront and ongoing costs against potential savings, productivity gains, and long-term benefits.

Example: Cross-Departmental DAM Selection

A global consumer brand assembled a cross-functional team to evaluate DAM systems, including representatives from marketing, creative, IT, legal, and finance. By gathering diverse perspectives, the team ensured the selected DAM met content management needs, supported technical infrastructure, complied with regulatory requirements, and demonstrated clear ROI potential.

7.2 Marketing's Perspective: Enhancing Efficiency and Campaign Agility

For the marketing team, a DAM system is essential for managing and distributing assets across campaigns and channels. Marketers need a DAM that allows them to locate, customize, and deploy assets quickly, especially as they aim to deliver timely, consistent, and personalized content.

- **Search and Metadata**: Marketers prioritize advanced search capabilities and customizable metadata fields, which enable them to find assets quickly, regardless of the size of the asset library.
- **Campaign Agility**: A DAM that integrates seamlessly with marketing platforms (such as CMS and social media scheduling tools) supports rapid content deployment, essential for executing agile, multi-channel campaigns.

Example: Marketing Needs in a DAM

A retail marketing team needs to launch seasonal campaigns rapidly, using assets stored within the DAM. By incorporating metadata that includes season, region, and product type, marketers can locate relevant assets efficiently, ensuring timely launches and consistent brand messaging.

7.3 Creative Team's Perspective: Supporting Asset Creation and Collaboration

The creative team relies on the DAM as a workspace for managing and sharing visual content. Their needs include version control, collaborative tools, and workflow automation to streamline asset development and feedback processes.

- **Version Control**: With versioning features, creatives can manage asset updates, track revisions, and revert to previous versions if needed, ensuring consistency and quality control.

- **Collaboration and Approval Workflows**: Creatives benefit from built-in collaboration tools, such as comments and annotations, and automated approval workflows that streamline the feedback and review process.

Example: Enhancing Creative Efficiency

A media company's creative team uses version control and collaborative workflows in their DAM to manage multiple revisions for video assets. The DAM tracks all changes, allowing team members to review and approve content seamlessly, saving time and avoiding version confusion.

7.4 IT's Perspective: Ensuring Security, Scalability, and Integrations

For the IT team, the focus is on ensuring that the DAM system integrates smoothly with the existing tech stack and meets organizational security standards. They also evaluate the DAM's scalability and reliability, ensuring it can handle future growth in content volume and usage.

- **Security and Compliance**: IT looks for DAMs that offer role-based access controls, multi-factor authentication, and encryption, providing the security measures necessary to protect sensitive content.

- **Technical Compatibility and Integrations**: IT evaluates whether the DAM can integrate with other tools and platforms, such as project management software, CMS, or analytics tools, which ensures a connected and streamlined marketing tech ecosystem.

Example: IT's Role in DAM Selection

A financial services firm's IT team evaluates DAMs based on security and compatibility with their current infrastructure. They prioritize features like advanced access controls and encryption, ensuring that the DAM meets regulatory and security requirements.

7.5 Legal's Perspective: Rights Management and Compliance

Legal teams play a vital role in DAM selection, particularly for organizations with regulatory or licensing requirements. They focus on ensuring the DAM can handle licensing restrictions, asset expiration, and rights management, which prevents unauthorized asset use and mitigates legal risks.

- **Rights Management**: Legal requires DAM features that track usage rights, including licensing terms, expiration dates, and restrictions by region or channel.
- **Audit Trails**: Legal teams value audit trails that provide a record of asset activity, which can be essential for compliance reporting and tracking usage history.

Example: Legal Requirements in DAM

An advertising agency's legal team uses the DAM's rights management features to monitor license agreements and ensure assets aren't used beyond their authorized scope. The DAM tracks expiration dates and provides alerts, allowing the team to renew or remove assets as needed.

7.6 Finance's Perspective: Evaluating ROI and Cost-Benefit Analysis

Finance departments evaluate DAM investment from a budgetary standpoint, analyzing potential cost savings, productivity gains, and ROI. Finance plays a key role in assessing the DAM's total cost of ownership, including setup, training, and maintenance, relative to its long-term benefits.

- **Cost Efficiency**: Finance teams calculate the potential for cost savings, such as reduced content duplication, faster campaign execution, and improved asset reuse.
- **ROI Metrics**: Finance will look at projected ROI, including time saved in asset management, reduced content creation costs, and the DAM's impact on overall marketing productivity.

Example: Financial Evaluation of DAM

A B2B company's finance team evaluates DAM systems by comparing setup and licensing costs against estimated time and cost savings. By projecting ROI based on the marketing team's anticipated efficiency gains, they determine the DAM's financial viability and potential to deliver long-term value.

7.7 Building a Collaborative Evaluation Team

With key stakeholders identified, the next step is to create a collaborative evaluation team that works together to define DAM requirements, review options, and make a final recommendation. Here's how to structure an effective evaluation team:

- **Define Roles and Responsibilities**: Each department's representative should understand their specific role in the evaluation process. Marketing might lead the requirements gathering, IT ensures technical alignment, and finance evaluates cost.
- **Conduct Regular Meetings**: Schedule regular meetings to review progress, discuss findings, and adjust the evaluation process as needed. Collaboration is key to ensuring all needs are considered.
- **Prioritize Requirements**: Create a prioritized list of DAM requirements based on input from each department, which helps guide the evaluation and ensures alignment with business goals.

Example: Structured Evaluation Team for DAM Selection

A global retailer's DAM evaluation team includes leads from marketing, creative, IT, legal, and finance, each contributing specific requirements and priorities. By collaborating on the evaluation criteria and holding weekly meetings, the team effectively narrows down potential DAM options, ensuring a well-rounded selection process.

Conclusion

Choosing the right DAM system requires input from various departments to ensure it aligns with organizational goals and meets the unique needs of each team. By involving key stakeholders, such as marketing, creative, IT, legal, and finance, organizations can evaluate DAM options holistically and build a strong case for investment. A collaborative evaluation team ensures that all perspectives are considered, paving the way for a DAM system that not only manages assets effectively but also drives efficiency, compliance, and strategic value across the organization.

In the next chapter, we'll discuss how to develop a selection criteria and evaluation framework, guiding your team in choosing the DAM that best aligns with your organization's requirements and long-term objectives.

Chapter 8: Developing a Selection Criteria and Evaluation Framework

Defining key factors such as scalability, customization, user interface, support, and security and outlining steps for creating and using a scoring system to evaluate different DAM options

TL;DR

Developing a DAM selection criteria and evaluation framework ensures a thorough, objective assessment of potential systems. Start by defining core criteria (like usability, search, and version control) and advanced features (such as AI tagging, automation, and analytics) that meet your organization's needs. Evaluate technical compatibility, security, scalability, and cost-effectiveness to understand long-term value. An evaluation matrix with weighted scores can help compare options objectively. Demos and trial runs allow teams to test essential workflows and gather feedback. By consolidating stakeholder input, you can make a well-informed recommendation that aligns with both team requirements and strategic goals.

With key stakeholders in place and their needs identified, the next step in selecting a Digital Asset Management (DAM) system is to establish clear evaluation criteria. Developing a well-defined framework helps guide the evaluation process, allowing your team to assess each DAM option against specific requirements and ensure it meets both operational needs and long-term strategic goals. In this chapter, we'll walk through how to build an evaluation framework, including criteria for core features, advanced capabilities, user experience, technical compatibility, and cost-effectiveness. With a structured approach, your team can make an informed decision and choose a DAM that delivers value across the organization.

8.1 Establishing Core Criteria for DAM Evaluation

The first step in creating a DAM evaluation framework is to establish core criteria that every potential solution should meet. These are the essential requirements that ensure the DAM will support your organization's primary needs. While specific criteria may vary by organization, the following categories are generally applicable:

- **User Interface and Usability**: The DAM should be user-friendly, with an intuitive interface that requires minimal training. Look for systems with a clean layout, straightforward navigation, and customizable views.
- **Search and Metadata**: Effective search and metadata capabilities are critical for locating assets quickly. Ensure the DAM supports metadata customization and offers robust search features, such as keyword, faceted, and AI-powered search.
- **Version Control and Asset Management**: Version control allows users to track changes, access previous iterations, and avoid version conflicts. Core asset management features should include tagging, organizing, and archiving.

Example: Defining Core Criteria for an E-Commerce Brand

An e-commerce brand prioritizes usability, advanced search functionality, and version control in their core criteria. These features ensure that marketing, creative, and merchandising teams can easily find, update, and manage assets across seasonal campaigns.

8.2 Advanced Criteria for Enhancing DAM Capabilities

Beyond core criteria, consider advanced features that provide added value, streamline workflows, and support scalability. Advanced criteria may include AI capabilities, workflow automation, integration with other tools, and analytics. These features can significantly enhance the DAM's functionality, making it a more powerful asset for the marketing and creative teams.

- **AI and Automation**: AI-driven features, such as automated tagging, image recognition, and content recommendations, reduce manual tasks and improve search accuracy. Workflow automation capabilities allow for streamlined approval processes and notifications.
- **Integration with Martech Stack**: The DAM should integrate with existing systems, such as CMS, CRM, social media scheduling, and project management tools, enabling seamless asset flow across the marketing ecosystem.
- **Analytics and Reporting**: Advanced DAMs provide insights into asset performance, usage trends, and user behavior, helping teams make data-driven content decisions and optimize asset utilization.

Example: Advanced Criteria for a Media Company

A media company values AI-driven tagging, integration with its CMS, and in-depth analytics in its DAM evaluation framework. These features streamline content creation and delivery, while analytics enable data-informed decisions for future campaigns.

8.3 Technical Criteria: Compatibility, Security, and Scalability

Technical compatibility is essential to ensure the DAM integrates seamlessly with your existing technology stack and meets organizational standards for security, compliance, and scalability. Technical criteria should be evaluated in collaboration with the IT team.

- **Compatibility with Existing Infrastructure**: The DAM should align with your organization's tech stack, supporting necessary integrations, APIs, and formats. It should also be compatible with file types commonly used in your workflows.
- **Security Features**: Key security features include role-based access control, multi-factor authentication, and data encryption. Consider whether the DAM complies with industry-specific security standards and regulations, such as GDPR or CCPA.
- **Scalability**: Ensure that the DAM can scale with your organization's growth. Scalability features include storage capacity, user limits, and support for high-volume asset libraries.

Example: Technical Evaluation for a Financial Services Firm

A financial services firm prioritizes data encryption, multi-factor authentication, and GDPR compliance as part of their technical criteria. By focusing on security and compliance, they ensure that sensitive client information remains protected.

8.4 Cost and ROI Evaluation

A DAM system represents a significant investment, so it's essential to evaluate costs carefully. While upfront costs are important, also consider ongoing costs, such as licensing, training, maintenance, and potential upgrades. Evaluate each DAM's pricing model, and calculate expected ROI by weighing productivity gains, time saved, and asset reusability.

- **Total Cost of Ownership (TCO)**: Look beyond initial costs and evaluate the long-term expenses, including training, support, storage, and any customizations that may be required.
- **ROI Potential**: Estimate the DAM's ROI by calculating potential time savings, reduction in asset duplication, and increased productivity. A DAM that enhances efficiency across multiple teams can yield significant long-term value.
- **Flexible Pricing Models**: Consider DAM providers that offer flexible pricing, such as tiered plans, to accommodate future growth or expansion without significant additional costs.

Example: ROI Evaluation for a B2B Software Company

A B2B software company calculates DAM ROI by estimating time saved in asset searches, reduction in duplicate asset creation, and faster campaign execution. These metrics help finance and leadership teams see the long-term value of DAM investment.

8.5 Building an Evaluation Matrix

An evaluation matrix is a structured tool for scoring each DAM system based on the criteria you've defined. By assigning weighted scores to each category, your team can objectively assess how well each DAM option meets your organization's requirements.

- **Assigning Weights**: Not all criteria carry equal importance, so assign weights to reflect your organization's priorities. For example, usability and search may have higher weights for marketing teams, while security and scalability may carry more weight for IT.
- **Scoring Each System**: Rate each DAM system on a scale (e.g., 1-5) for each criterion. Multiply each score by its weight to calculate a total score for each system.
- **Comparing Results**: Use the total scores to compare DAM systems. This matrix provides a clear, visual way to see which options best align with your organization's needs.

Example: Using an Evaluation Matrix

A global fashion brand creates an evaluation matrix with criteria like usability, AI features, integrations, and security. By assigning higher weights to usability and integrations, the team prioritizes solutions that will be easy to adopt and support their existing tech ecosystem.

8.6 Conducting Demos and Trial Runs

After narrowing down DAM options using your evaluation matrix, the next step is to conduct demos and trial runs. A hands-on experience allows users from each department to test core and advanced features, providing insights that a theoretical evaluation may not capture.

- **User Feedback Sessions**: Organize demo sessions for each team, allowing them to explore relevant features and provide feedback on usability and functionality.
- **Testing Key Workflows**: Have users test essential workflows, such as uploading, tagging, searching, and sharing assets. This helps reveal any usability issues or potential bottlenecks.
- **Assessing User Experience**: Observe how easily users navigate the interface and perform tasks, as this will impact adoption and ease of use after implementation.

Example: Trial Run Insights for a Retail Brand

A retail brand's marketing and creative teams participate in a DAM demo, testing asset retrieval, tagging, and collaboration workflows.

Their feedback highlights potential friction points, helping the team refine their selection criteria and make an informed final choice.

8.7 Collecting Stakeholder Feedback and Finalizing Recommendations

Once demos and trial runs are complete, collect feedback from all stakeholders to finalize the DAM recommendation. Consolidating insights from each department ensures that the selected DAM will meet both individual team needs and broader organizational objectives.

- **Survey Stakeholders**: Use a survey or structured feedback form to collect input on each DAM's strengths, weaknesses, and alignment with department-specific requirements.
- **Review and Adjust the Evaluation Matrix**: Update the evaluation matrix based on new insights from the demos and trial runs, adjusting scores if necessary.
- **Compile Final Recommendations**: Summarize the evaluation results and feedback in a final recommendation document, including the top DAM choice, supporting data, and the reasons for your recommendation.

Example: Collaborative Decision-Making for DAM Selection

After reviewing feedback from all teams, a multinational corporation compiles a final recommendation for their chosen DAM. By documenting each team's feedback and aligning it with the evaluation matrix results, they present a strong case for their selected system to leadership.

Conclusion

Developing a clear, structured evaluation framework for DAM selection ensures that each option is thoroughly assessed and meets your organization's specific needs. By defining core and advanced criteria, evaluating technical compatibility, and considering cost-effectiveness, you create a well-rounded approach to DAM selection. Incorporating an evaluation matrix, demos, and feedback from stakeholders further strengthens the process, leading to a DAM solution that supports efficiency, scalability, and strategic value across the organization.

In the next chapter, we'll explore the steps for implementing a DAM, from configuring the system and setting up workflows to training users and launching it successfully within your organization.

Chapter 9: Conducting Demos and Trial Runs

Best practices for running trials or demos to ensure all stakeholders' needs are met and tips for using trial data to make an informed decision.

TL;DR

A successful DAM implementation involves strategic planning, configuration, and user training. Start by creating a clear project roadmap with defined phases and milestones. Configure metadata and taxonomy to ensure easy asset search and organization, then prepare for data migration by cleaning and organizing existing files. Set up workflows for

efficient asset approval and assign permissions to control access. Role-specific training and onboarding sessions promote user adoption, while a phased rollout helps address issues early. Post-launch, monitor usage metrics and gather feedback to make iterative improvements, ensuring the DAM remains valuable and aligned with organizational needs.

Once you've selected a Digital Asset Management (DAM) system that meets your organization's needs, the next step is implementation. A successful DAM implementation requires more than just technical setup—it involves strategic planning, collaboration across departments, and thorough training to ensure a smooth transition. In this chapter, we'll outline the key steps for implementing a DAM, from defining a project roadmap and configuring metadata to onboarding users and promoting adoption. By approaching implementation thoughtfully, you can maximize the DAM's impact, streamline workflows, and ensure that your team is well-prepared to use the system effectively.

9.1 Defining a Clear Project Roadmap

A detailed project roadmap is essential for keeping the DAM implementation process on track. It outlines the steps needed to configure, test, and launch the system, establishing a timeline with key milestones to ensure timely progress.

- **Project Phases**: Break down the implementation process into phases, such as configuration, data migration, user training, and go-live. Each phase should have specific goals and deliverables.
- **Milestones and Deadlines**: Set clear milestones to measure progress and hold the implementation team accountable. Common milestones include finalizing metadata structure, completing a test run, and training the initial user group.
- **Assigning Responsibilities**: Define roles for each team member involved in the implementation. This might include IT staff for technical setup, marketing and creative leads for content organization, and project managers for overall coordination.

Example: Roadmap for a Retail Brand's DAM Implementation

A retail brand's DAM implementation roadmap includes phases for system configuration, metadata setup, and pilot testing. The roadmap sets milestones for completing each stage, ensuring timely progress and allowing the project manager to address any delays or obstacles.

9.2 Configuring Metadata and Taxonomy

Metadata and taxonomy are foundational elements of a DAM system, as they define how assets are organized and searched. Proper configuration of metadata fields, tags, and taxonomy ensures that assets are easy to locate, enhancing efficiency and usability.

- **Metadata Field Selection**: Work with each department to identify relevant metadata fields, such as asset type, campaign name, region, and licensing information. These fields should support specific search and filtering needs.
- **Establishing a Taxonomy**: Define a clear taxonomy, or organizational structure, for your assets. For example, assets could be organized by categories like "Product Images," "Social Media," and "Campaigns."
- **Standardizing Tags and Keywords**: Standardize keywords to maintain consistency across assets. This includes establishing naming conventions for tags and creating guidelines for users to follow when uploading assets.

Example: Metadata and Taxonomy Setup for a Healthcare Organization

A healthcare organization configures metadata fields like "department," "region," and "usage restrictions" to ensure compliant asset usage. Their taxonomy groups assets by content type, making it easy for staff to locate approved materials for specific campaigns.

9.3 Preparing for Data Migration

Data migration involves transferring assets from existing storage locations into the new DAM. Proper preparation ensures a seamless migration process, preserving asset quality, metadata, and organizational structure.

- **Inventory of Existing Assets**: Begin by conducting an inventory of all existing digital assets, identifying which files should be transferred to the DAM.
- **Cleaning and Organizing Files**: Remove duplicates, outdated assets, and irrelevant files. Clean data makes the DAM more effective, reducing clutter and improving searchability.
- **Mapping Metadata**: Map existing metadata from current storage systems to the DAM. If metadata was inconsistent, take the opportunity to standardize tags and fields during migration.

Example: Streamlining Data Migration for a Media Company

A media company preparing for data migration organizes files by relevance and updates metadata to align with DAM requirements. By cleaning up their asset library, they streamline the migration process and make the DAM easier to navigate.

9.4 Developing User Workflows and Approval Processes

Configuring workflows and approval processes in the DAM allows users to collaborate efficiently and ensures assets go through the necessary review stages. These workflows can be tailored to specific team needs, reducing delays and maintaining quality control.

- **Setting Up Review and Approval Workflows**: Define workflows for common processes, such as new asset creation and campaign content review. Automated notifications can alert team members when their input or approval is required.
- **Task Assignments and Permissions**: Assign specific tasks to different roles, ensuring that each user knows their responsibilities within the workflow. Permissions can limit access to sensitive content, ensuring security and compliance.

Example: Approval Workflow for a Global Brand

A global brand uses an approval workflow in their DAM to streamline content review for regional campaigns. Marketing managers receive automatic notifications to review assets before they're released in their markets, ensuring brand consistency and regional compliance.

9.5 Conducting Training and Onboarding Sessions

Training is essential to ensure users understand how to navigate and use the DAM effectively. A well-structured onboarding program reduces confusion, increases adoption, and helps users realize the DAM's full potential from day one.

- **Role-Specific Training**: Tailor training sessions to each user group's specific needs. For example, creative teams might focus on

asset upload and version control, while marketers learn search and tagging.
- **Creating User Guides and Documentation**: Develop comprehensive user guides that explain key functionalities, workflows, and best practices. Documentation ensures users have a reference when they encounter questions or challenges.
- **Ongoing Support and Refresher Training**: Provide ongoing support through help desks or dedicated contacts for DAM questions. Consider offering refresher training as new features are introduced or user needs evolve.

Example: Structured Training for a Non-Profit Organization

A non-profit organizes role-specific training for their DAM users, including a creative session on version control and a marketing session on search and tagging. This approach increases confidence and ensures each team can use the DAM to its full potential.

9.6 Launching the DAM and Promoting User Adoption

The final step in implementation is to launch the DAM to the broader organization and promote user adoption. A successful launch strategy includes a phased rollout, internal marketing, and continuous monitoring to address any issues.

- **Phased Rollout**: Consider launching the DAM in phases, starting with a pilot group to identify and address potential issues before organization-wide deployment.
- **Internal Marketing and Engagement**: Promote the DAM internally with communication channels like email newsletters, demos, or "how-to" videos. Highlight benefits, such as time savings and ease of use, to encourage adoption.
- **Collecting Feedback Post-Launch**: After launch, gather feedback from users on any challenges or improvements. This feedback helps you refine the system, ensuring that it meets evolving needs.

Example: Phased Rollout for a Financial Institution

A financial institution launches its DAM with a phased rollout, starting with a small pilot team. After collecting and acting on initial feedback, they expand access to the entire organization, promoting the DAM's benefits through workshops and demos to encourage adoption.

9.7 Monitoring Usage and Optimizing the DAM

DAM implementation doesn't end with launch; ongoing monitoring is essential to ensure continued success and adapt the system to changing needs. Tracking usage metrics and gathering regular feedback enables continuous improvement.

- **Tracking Key Metrics**: Monitor metrics like asset views, search frequency, and user activity to gauge how the DAM is being used.

Metrics can reveal underutilized features or popular assets, informing future optimizations.
- **User Feedback and Iterative Improvements**: Periodically survey users to gather feedback on DAM functionality and usability. Use this input to make iterative improvements, such as adjusting workflows or enhancing metadata.
- **Updating Metadata and Taxonomy**: As the asset library grows, regularly review and update metadata and taxonomy to keep the DAM organized and relevant.

Example: Continuous Optimization for a Technology Company

A technology company regularly reviews DAM usage metrics and surveys users to identify improvement areas. By adjusting workflows and expanding metadata fields, they keep the DAM aligned with team needs and ensure it remains a valuable resource.

Conclusion

A successful DAM implementation requires careful planning, structured training, and continuous optimization. By following a clear roadmap, configuring metadata, migrating data, and setting up workflows, you can ensure the DAM meets organizational needs from the start. Training and onboarding are essential for promoting user adoption, while a phased launch and ongoing feedback loop help you refine the system post-launch. With this comprehensive approach, your organization can maximize the value of its DAM investment and achieve greater efficiency, collaboration, and brand consistency.

In the next chapter, we'll explore best practices for ongoing DAM management, including strategies for governance, content lifecycle management, and optimizing the DAM as your organization evolves.

Part 4: Implementing a DAM

Implementing and configuring a DAM system is only the beginning. To realize its full potential, organizations must continually evaluate, refine, and adapt their DAM as needs evolve. Part 4 focuses on strategies for assessing your DAM's effectiveness, measuring ROI, and ensuring that it keeps pace with both technological advancements and organizational growth. By setting benchmarks, gathering user feedback, and analyzing performance metrics, you can identify opportunities for improvement and optimize workflows to increase DAM value over time.

This part also explores how to align DAM with changing business goals, accommodate new types of assets, and scale effectively as your team expands. With a proactive approach to assessment and evolution, your DAM can remain an adaptable, high-performing tool that enhances collaboration, supports brand consistency, and delivers long-term strategic value.

Chapter 10: Planning for Implementation

Covering timeline creation, setting milestones, and change management considerations.

TL;DR

Effective DAM configuration is key to maximizing efficiency and usability. Start by setting up consistent metadata and an intuitive taxonomy to make assets easy to find. Organize folders and establish clear naming conventions to streamline navigation. Configure permissions based on user roles to protect sensitive content and enable collaborative workflows with automated approvals and task assignments. Offering preset download options ensures assets are optimized for various channels, while analytics help track asset performance and user engagement. Regularly review and optimize your DAM configuration to keep it aligned with evolving organizational needs, ensuring lasting value and efficiency.

Proper configuration is at the core of an effective Digital Asset Management (DAM) system. A well-configured DAM doesn't just store assets—it enhances productivity, ensures brand consistency, and empowers teams to locate and use assets seamlessly. Configuring your DAM thoughtfully from the start, with an eye on user needs and organizational goals, can significantly reduce time spent searching for assets, simplify workflows, and make it easier to manage content across departments. In this chapter, we'll cover key aspects of DAM configuration, including metadata, taxonomy, folder structure, and permissions, as well as tips for optimizing each element to support efficiency and ease of use.

10.1 Setting Up Metadata for Effective Search and Organization

Metadata is essential for organizing and finding assets in the DAM. Without consistent, well-structured metadata, assets can quickly become difficult to locate, which reduces the DAM's effectiveness. Configuring metadata fields to reflect your team's needs enables precise searchability and streamlined access.

- **Choosing Metadata Fields**: Collaborate with different teams to determine relevant metadata fields, such as asset type, campaign, product category, and usage rights. Ensure these fields align with the needs of end users.
- **Standardizing Metadata Formats**: Consistent metadata formats (e.g., date formats, naming conventions) prevent confusion and improve search results. For example, establish a standard format for naming campaigns or products to keep tags uniform.
- **Mandatory vs. Optional Fields**: Set mandatory fields for critical metadata, such as asset type and campaign, to ensure every asset has essential tags. Optional fields can capture additional details without overwhelming users during upload.

Example: Metadata Configuration for a Hospitality Brand

A hospitality brand sets up mandatory metadata fields like "property location," "season," and "room type" to make it easy for users to find assets relevant to specific properties or seasons. This configuration ensures that marketing teams can quickly locate images for regional campaigns.

10.2 Creating an Intuitive Taxonomy and Folder Structure

A well-organized taxonomy and folder structure help users navigate the DAM effortlessly. Taxonomy defines the categories, subcategories, and relationships between assets, while folder structure organizes assets into logical, easy-to-find groups. Thoughtful taxonomy and folder design make assets easy to find, especially for users unfamiliar with specific file names or keywords.

- **Define Categories and Subcategories**: Begin with broad categories like "Campaign Assets," "Product Images," and "Social Media," then create subcategories based on asset type, date, or target audience. This structure should be intuitive and align with the organization's workflow.
- **Avoid Over-Complicated Structures**: Keep the taxonomy simple and streamlined. Overly complex structures can make assets harder to find and lead to user frustration.
- **Establish Naming Conventions**: Set guidelines for folder and asset names to maintain consistency. Naming conventions prevent duplication and enable users to identify assets without needing to open each file.

Example: Folder Structure for a Consumer Goods Company

A consumer goods company organizes its DAM with main folders for "Product Launches," "Campaigns," and "Social Media," each containing subfolders by year and quarter. This structure allows users to find relevant assets quickly, even as the library grows.

10.3 Defining Permissions and Access Control for Security

Configuring permissions and access control is crucial for protecting sensitive content and ensuring assets are used appropriately. Permissions settings determine who can view, edit, download, or share assets, allowing organizations to manage access based on user roles and responsibilities.

- **Role-Based Permissions**: Set permissions based on user roles, such as "view-only" for general staff, "edit" for creatives, and "approval" for managers. This ensures each user has access to the right assets without compromising security.
- **Limit Access to Sensitive Content**: For assets with restricted usage (e.g., licensed content, confidential images), set access limitations to specific users or departments. Restricted access helps ensure assets are only used by authorized personnel.
- **Audit and Monitor Access**: Regularly audit permissions to ensure they remain aligned with user roles. Monitoring access can also help identify and address potential security risks.

Example: Permissions Structure for a Pharmaceutical Company

A pharmaceutical company configures permissions to limit access to research and product assets, allowing only authorized marketing and compliance teams to view or edit sensitive materials. This structure helps them meet regulatory requirements and protects confidential information.

10.4 Configuring Automated Workflows for Collaboration

Automated workflows enhance collaboration by guiding assets through review and approval stages. Configuring workflows to match team needs ensures assets go through appropriate checkpoints before final use, streamlining communication and preventing bottlenecks.

- **Approval Workflows**: Set up approval workflows for commonly used processes, such as campaign asset creation or content updates. Notifications alert relevant team members to review, approve, or make changes, reducing delays.
- **Task Assignments**: Assign specific tasks to team members within the DAM, such as tagging, metadata entry, or quality checks. Task assignments help users understand their responsibilities and keep workflows on track.
- **Automated Notifications**: Enable notifications for workflow stages, such as when an asset is awaiting approval or has been approved. This keeps stakeholders informed and minimizes the need for follow-up emails.

Example: Workflow for a Retailer's Social Media Team

A retailer's social media team uses an approval workflow to review and approve social assets. The DAM automatically notifies marketing managers when content is ready for review, allowing them to approve or request revisions. This automation keeps content aligned with brand guidelines and accelerates posting timelines.

10.5 Enabling Download Options and Format Variants

Configuring download options allows users to access assets in different sizes or formats, depending on the intended use. Predefined download formats ensure assets are optimized for specific channels, saving time and maintaining quality across platforms.

- **Preset Download Sizes and Formats**: Set up commonly used download options, such as high-resolution for print and web-optimized for online use. Users can select the appropriate format without manual resizing.
- **On-the-Fly Conversion**: Some DAMs support on-the-fly conversion, allowing users to download assets in custom sizes or formats directly from the platform. This feature can save time and increase flexibility.
- **Limit Access to Original Files**: Limit access to high-resolution files if only a few users require them, which helps prevent accidental overuse of large files and preserves storage.

Example: Predefined Download Options for an E-Commerce Company

An e-commerce company sets up download presets for product images, allowing team members to download images optimized for email, website, and social media. This configuration ensures consistency across channels and saves time in resizing.

10.6 Setting Up Analytics for Performance Tracking

Analytics provide valuable insights into how assets are used, which teams are most active, and which assets perform well. Configuring analytics allows you to monitor DAM usage, identify popular assets, and gather data to support ongoing optimization.

- **Asset Usage Metrics**: Track metrics like asset views, downloads, and usage frequency. Usage data reveals which assets are most valuable, helping guide future content creation.
- **User Engagement**: Monitor user activity to understand how different teams interact with the DAM. If specific features are underutilized, consider additional training or adjustments to improve engagement.
- **Campaign-Specific Analytics**: Link assets to campaigns to track their impact on campaign performance. Campaign-level analytics

help you see which visuals resonate with audiences and inform future marketing strategies.

Example: Analytics Setup for a B2B Company

A B2B company configures its DAM analytics to track asset usage by sales and marketing teams. By analyzing which assets are most frequently downloaded for client presentations, they identify the types of content that resonate most with their audience and prioritize similar asset creation.

10.7 Optimizing Your DAM Configuration Over Time

DAM configuration is not a one-time setup; it requires periodic optimization as the organization's needs evolve. Regularly reviewing and updating your DAM's metadata, permissions, workflows, and taxonomy ensures the system remains efficient and aligned with business goals.

- **Annual Metadata Review**: Schedule regular metadata reviews to update fields, remove outdated tags, and adjust formats based on feedback from users.
- **User Feedback and Iteration**: Collect feedback from DAM users to identify areas for improvement, such as new workflow requirements or additional metadata fields.
- **Expanding Taxonomy for Growth**: As the DAM grows, adjust taxonomy to accommodate new categories, subcategories, or asset

types. Updating the taxonomy ensures assets remain organized and easy to find.

Example: Continuous Optimization for a Non-Profit

A non-profit organization reviews its DAM configuration every six months, adding new metadata fields and adjusting permissions as their asset library expands. This iterative approach keeps the DAM relevant and effective, supporting ongoing campaigns and fundraising efforts.

Conclusion

Proper DAM configuration is essential to maximize efficiency, streamline workflows, and ensure assets are organized and accessible. By setting up clear metadata and taxonomy, structuring permissions, establishing workflows, and enabling analytics, you create a DAM that not only stores assets but actively supports your team's productivity and brand consistency. Continuous optimization keeps the DAM aligned with evolving organizational needs, making it a valuable tool for both day-to-day operations and strategic marketing goals.

In the next chapter, we'll explore the training and onboarding process, offering best practices to ensure your team is confident and capable of using the DAM to its fullest potential.

Chapter 11: Configuring Your DAM to Maximize Efficiency

Exploring the importance of metadata standards, folder structures, and taxonomy setup and strategies to optimize configuration for brand consistency and ease of use.

TL;DR

Successful DAM adoption relies on effective training and onboarding. Tailor training to each user role, providing marketing, creative, IT, and compliance teams with relevant guidance. Develop comprehensive onboarding materials, including user guides, video tutorials, and troubleshooting

FAQs, to support independent learning. Initial training sessions should include hands-on workshops and Q&A time, while ongoing support can be provided through office hours, helpdesks, and a knowledge base. Encourage engagement with internal marketing and recognize active users. Track success through usage metrics and feedback to refine training, ensuring users feel confident and maximizing DAM's value across the organization.

A well-configured DAM system is only as effective as the people using it. Proper training and onboarding are essential for ensuring that users understand how to navigate the DAM, utilize its features, and integrate it into their daily workflows. A thorough onboarding program promotes early adoption, reduces confusion, and sets users up to leverage the DAM to its fullest potential. In this chapter, we'll outline best practices for training different user groups, developing clear onboarding materials, and fostering an ongoing support system to ensure that your team feels confident and capable of using the DAM effectively.

11.1 Identifying Training Needs by User Role

DAM users often come from different departments with unique responsibilities, so it's important to tailor training to address the needs of each group. This approach ensures that every user learns the specific DAM functionalities relevant to their role, making the training sessions more engaging and practical.

- **Marketing and Content Teams**: These teams require training on asset search, tagging, download options, and campaign-specific workflows. They may also benefit from learning how to use analytics to track asset performance.
- **Creative and Design Teams**: Creatives need to understand workflows related to uploading, version control, and metadata entry. Training should emphasize version management, collaborative feedback tools, and approval processes.
- **IT and Compliance**: IT teams need training on security settings, permissions, and integrations, while compliance teams benefit from understanding rights management, licensing, and audit trails.
- **Leadership and Management**: Managers may not use the DAM daily, but they should know how to access usage metrics and monitor team productivity. High-level training can focus on reporting, asset usage insights, and workflow approvals.

Example: Role-Specific Training for a Publishing Company

A publishing company develops tailored training sessions for their marketing, creative, and compliance teams, focusing on each team's specific DAM interactions. By aligning training with job functions, they ensure each team can use the DAM efficiently and confidently in their daily tasks.

11.2 Developing Clear and Comprehensive Onboarding Materials

Onboarding materials provide users with guidance they can reference as they get accustomed to the DAM. By creating detailed guides, how-to videos, and step-by-step instructions, you equip users with resources to support independent learning and reduce reliance on IT support.

- **User Guides and Manuals**: Comprehensive user guides should cover essential topics like uploading assets, searching with metadata, and managing permissions. Structure guides by topic and include screenshots to make instructions clear.
- **Video Tutorials and Walkthroughs**: Short, task-specific videos are ideal for visual learners. Consider creating tutorials that cover tasks such as uploading assets, tagging, and navigating workflows, allowing users to follow along at their own pace.
- **FAQs and Troubleshooting Guides**: Address common questions and potential challenges in an FAQ document. Include troubleshooting steps for common issues, which can reduce helpdesk requests and empower users to solve problems independently.

Example: Onboarding Materials for a Non-Profit Organization

A non-profit creates video tutorials on tasks like uploading photos and searching for event materials. They also provide a troubleshooting guide with common questions about metadata and permissions, helping staff quickly resolve issues and stay productive.

11.3 Structuring Initial Training Sessions

Initial training sessions are an opportunity to introduce users to the DAM, demonstrate its key functionalities, and establish foundational skills. These sessions can be held in person, remotely, or as a combination of both, depending on your team's location and preferences.

- **Hands-On Workshops**: Interactive workshops allow users to practice tasks with live guidance. Workshops are particularly helpful for learning search functions, asset tagging, and approval workflows.
- **Role-Specific Sessions**: Divide training sessions by user role, focusing on the features most relevant to each group. For example, marketing teams can practice asset retrieval and download options, while creative teams focus on version control and collaboration tools.
- **Q&A Sessions**: Allow time for questions and answers in each session, encouraging users to voice any concerns or clarify uncertainties. This also helps trainers identify topics that may require further focus.

Example: Hands-On Training for a Financial Institution

A financial institution hosts role-specific, hands-on workshops for their DAM users. Marketing teams practice searching and downloading approved assets, while compliance teams focus on rights management and licensing features, ensuring everyone gains relevant skills.

11.4 Creating an Ongoing Support System

Training doesn't end with the initial sessions; an effective DAM adoption strategy includes ongoing support. Establishing a system for continuous assistance, updates, and feedback ensures that users have a reliable support network as they become more comfortable with the DAM.

- **Helpdesk and Dedicated Support Contacts**: Designate a helpdesk or dedicated DAM support contact that users can reach out to with questions. This ensures that users always have someone to turn to for guidance.
- **Office Hours and Refresher Sessions**: Schedule regular office hours or refresher training sessions where users can drop in for additional help. These sessions can cover new features, address common challenges, or provide role-specific training as needed.
- **User Community and Knowledge Base**: Create a user community or online knowledge base where team members can ask questions, share tips, and discuss best practices. A knowledge base with searchable articles offers a self-service option for common questions.

Example: Support System for an E-Commerce Brand

An e-commerce brand establishes a monthly office hour for DAM support, where users can ask questions or request personalized help. They also set up a knowledge base with articles on tasks like asset tagging and troubleshooting, creating a reliable support network for users.

11.5 Promoting Engagement and Encouraging Adoption

Promoting the DAM and its benefits to the team fosters enthusiasm and helps ensure widespread adoption. Internal communications and incentives can encourage users to explore the DAM and integrate it into their daily workflows.

- **Internal Marketing Campaign**: Launch an internal marketing campaign to introduce the DAM, showcasing its benefits and providing "how-to" guides for common tasks. Use newsletters, email updates, and videos to keep users informed.
- **Incentives and Recognition**: Recognize power users and those who adopt the DAM enthusiastically. Consider implementing rewards, such as shout-outs in team meetings, for employees who consistently use and promote the DAM.
- **User Feedback and Iteration**: Regularly collect user feedback on the DAM experience and make iterative improvements based on this input. Listening to users helps address challenges and keeps the DAM aligned with team needs.

Example: Engagement Strategy for a Consumer Goods Company

A consumer goods company promotes the DAM through an email newsletter series, showcasing tips, user success stories, and new features. By recognizing early adopters and gathering user feedback, they build excitement and drive consistent usage.

11.6 Measuring Training Success and Adoption

Tracking training success and DAM adoption rates helps you assess whether users feel comfortable with the DAM and are integrating it into their workflows. By gathering usage metrics and soliciting feedback, you can identify any gaps in training and continue to support users effectively.

- **Usage Metrics**: Track DAM usage metrics, such as asset searches, uploads, and downloads, to gauge adoption. High activity rates indicate successful integration, while low usage may signal a need for additional training.
- **User Feedback Surveys**: Conduct surveys after initial training and at regular intervals to gather feedback on the DAM experience. Ask users about ease of use, challenges, and suggestions for improvement.
- **Completion of Key Tasks**: Assess users' ability to complete key tasks, like searching for assets or managing workflows, as a

measure of training effectiveness. Consider setting up test scenarios to evaluate user proficiency.

Example: Measuring Success for a B2B Software Company

A B2B software company measures DAM adoption by tracking user activity metrics and conducting a post-training survey. The survey results reveal that users need additional guidance on metadata tagging, prompting a refresher session that improves confidence and usage rates.

Conclusion

Effective training and onboarding are critical for DAM adoption, ensuring that users feel confident navigating the system and integrating it into their daily workflows. By providing role-specific training, comprehensive onboarding materials, and ongoing support, you create a strong foundation for DAM usage across the organization. Encouraging engagement through internal promotion and tracking success with metrics and feedback enables continuous improvement, maximizing the DAM's value. With a well-trained team, your DAM can fulfill its potential as a powerful tool for efficiency, collaboration, and brand consistency.

In the next chapter, we'll explore best practices for managing the DAM long-term, including strategies for governance, lifecycle management, and optimizing the DAM as your organization evolves.

Chapter 12: Training and Onboarding Your Team

Including training tips to help different user groups (marketers, creatives, managers) use the DAM effectively as well as tips on creating user guides, conducting workshops, and setting up ongoing support.

TL;DR

Ongoing DAM management ensures that the system remains effective, organized, and adaptable. Establish governance with clear roles and guidelines to maintain consistency, and implement lifecycle management practices to prevent clutter from outdated assets. Regularly update metadata and taxonomy to reflect changing needs and track usage metrics to monitor engagement and optimize configuration. Continuous training, user feedback, and a scalable setup support long-term adoption and effectiveness. By following these best practices, you can maintain a DAM that grows with your organization, driving productivity and supporting collaboration over time.

Implementing a DAM is only the first step; ensuring its long-term success requires ongoing management and optimization. As your organization grows, so will the volume and diversity of digital assets, making it essential to regularly review, update, and refine your DAM system. By following best practices for DAM governance, content lifecycle management, user engagement, and performance tracking, you can ensure that your DAM continues to serve as an effective and adaptable tool. In this chapter, we'll explore strategies for keeping your DAM organized, user-friendly, and aligned with evolving business needs.

12.1 Establishing DAM Governance and Ownership

A strong governance framework is essential for maintaining DAM quality and consistency over time. Governance policies define roles, responsibilities, and standards for asset management, ensuring that your DAM remains organized, compliant, and aligned with organizational goals.

- **Define Ownership and Roles**: Designate a DAM administrator responsible for overall system oversight, maintenance, and updates. Define additional roles, such as content curators, metadata managers, and department-specific users, to support daily operations.
- **Set Standards and Guidelines**: Develop guidelines for metadata, taxonomy, and file naming conventions to ensure consistency. Clear standards make it easier for users to navigate the DAM and locate assets efficiently.
- **Regularly Review Permissions**: Periodically audit user permissions to confirm that they're aligned with current roles and responsibilities, removing access for users who no longer need it to maintain security.

Example: Governance Framework for a Healthcare Organization

A healthcare organization assigns a DAM administrator and department-level content curators to manage the system. They establish guidelines for metadata, permissions, and asset tagging, ensuring compliance with healthcare regulations and consistent asset management practices.

12.2 Managing Content Lifecycle and Archiving

Efficient lifecycle management prevents the DAM from becoming cluttered with outdated or irrelevant assets. By implementing content lifecycle policies, you can keep the system organized, relevant, and useful for end users.

- **Define Asset Lifecycles**: Identify the stages of an asset's lifecycle—from creation and active use to archiving or deletion. For example, campaign-specific assets may be archived after the campaign ends, while evergreen content remains active.
- **Automate Expiration Dates and Archiving**: Use DAM features that allow you to set expiration dates for assets, automatically moving them to an archive when they're no longer needed. This reduces clutter and ensures users only see current content.
- **Establish an Archiving Process**: Develop an archiving strategy that keeps older assets accessible but separate from active files. Archived assets can be retrieved if needed, but they won't appear in general searches or active folders.

Example: Lifecycle Management for a Consumer Goods Brand

A consumer goods brand sets expiration dates for seasonal campaign assets, moving them to an archive six months after the campaign ends. Evergreen product images remain active, ensuring that users can easily find assets for current products.

12.3 Updating Metadata and Taxonomy as Needs Evolve

Metadata and taxonomy need regular updates to reflect new campaigns, products, and business requirements. Periodically reviewing and refining these elements keeps the DAM organized and ensures assets are easy to find as the organization's needs change.

- **Conduct Regular Metadata Reviews**: Schedule periodic reviews of metadata fields to update tags, remove outdated fields, and adjust formats based on feedback. This helps maintain relevance and accuracy as the asset library grows.
- **Expand Taxonomy for New Categories**: As your content needs expand, update taxonomy with new categories or subcategories, such as new product lines or campaign types. This flexibility keeps the DAM structured and aligned with user needs.
- **User Feedback on Taxonomy**: Solicit feedback from DAM users on taxonomy and metadata, as they may have insights into what makes assets easier or harder to locate. This feedback can guide adjustments to improve searchability and user satisfaction.

Example: Metadata Update for a Financial Services Firm

A financial services firm updates its taxonomy annually to reflect new service lines and regulatory changes. By adding new tags and subcategories, they ensure that users can locate assets relevant to evolving services and compliance requirements.

12.4 Monitoring DAM Usage and User Engagement

Regularly monitoring usage metrics helps you understand how the DAM is performing, identify popular assets, and determine which features are underused. Tracking engagement helps you tailor the DAM to meet users' needs and address potential barriers to usage.

- **Track Asset Usage Metrics**: Monitor metrics like asset views, downloads, and shares to identify which assets are most valuable. Usage patterns reveal high-demand content and can inform future asset creation.
- **Analyze User Activity**: Assess user activity by department or role to see which teams engage most frequently with the DAM. If certain teams have low engagement, consider additional training or resources to improve adoption.
- **Adjust Based on Insights**: Use analytics insights to optimize DAM configuration, such as adding shortcuts to popular assets or reworking workflows for frequently accessed content.

Example: User Engagement Analysis for a B2B Tech Company

A B2B tech company tracks which assets are downloaded most frequently by the sales and marketing teams. By analyzing these patterns, they prioritize similar content for future campaigns, increasing relevance and supporting high-impact initiatives.

12.5 Continuously Training and Supporting Users

Training shouldn't stop after initial onboarding; continuous training keeps users updated on new features, best practices, and evolving workflows. A strong support system ensures users stay engaged and confident in their DAM usage.

- **Refresher Training and New Feature Demos**: Offer refresher training sessions periodically to cover underused features and demonstrate new capabilities. This keeps users informed and helps them get the most out of the DAM.
- **Role-Specific Updates**: Tailor updates and training to specific user groups based on their DAM usage patterns. For example, creatives may benefit from new workflow tips, while marketers might appreciate insights on metadata tagging and search techniques.
- **Accessible Support Channels**: Provide easy access to support through helpdesks, office hours, or an online knowledge base. An accessible support network ensures users can get help whenever they need it, encouraging consistent DAM use.

Example: Ongoing Training for a Media Company

A media company hosts quarterly DAM webinars, covering new features and fielding questions from users. This ongoing training keeps the team updated and promotes DAM adoption, reducing the need for one-on-one support.

12.6 Gathering and Acting on User Feedback

User feedback is invaluable for continuous DAM optimization. By gathering insights directly from users, you can identify areas for improvement, optimize workflows, and ensure the DAM remains aligned with changing organizational needs.

- **Regular User Surveys**: Conduct surveys or focus groups with DAM users to gather feedback on usability, feature requests, and any pain points they experience. Surveys provide a structured way to capture user perspectives.
- **Review and Implement Feedback**: Review feedback regularly and prioritize actionable improvements. This could include refining workflows, adjusting permissions, or adding new metadata fields to meet user needs.
- **Communicate Updates Based on Feedback**: When implementing changes based on feedback, inform users of the updates and how they enhance the DAM experience. This reinforces the value of their input and encourages ongoing engagement.

Example: Feedback Loop for a Retailer's DAM

A retailer conducts a semi-annual survey to collect feedback on their DAM. Based on user requests, they add new search filters and streamline metadata fields, improving the overall user experience and making it easier to find assets.

12.7 Planning for DAM Scalability and Growth

As your organization and asset library grow, ensure that the DAM remains scalable and adaptable. Planning for growth involves managing storage, expanding taxonomy, and preparing the DAM to handle larger asset volumes and user activity.

- **Assess Storage Needs**: Monitor storage usage to ensure sufficient capacity as new assets are added. If asset volume grows rapidly, consider upgrading storage options or implementing more rigorous archiving to manage space.
- **Future-Proof Metadata and Taxonomy**: Keep metadata and taxonomy flexible to accommodate new products, campaigns, and organizational changes. Build in room for additional categories and subcategories as needed.
- **Prepare for Increased User Activity**: As more users access the DAM, prepare for higher demand on workflows and permissions. Regularly evaluate system performance and scalability to ensure the DAM can support growing usage.

Example: Scaling for a Non-Profit's DAM

A non-profit organization anticipates rapid growth in digital content for future campaigns. They increase storage capacity and expand metadata fields to manage a larger volume of assets, ensuring that their DAM can support evolving needs.

Conclusion

Ongoing DAM management and optimization are essential for maintaining an organized, efficient, and scalable system that serves your team's needs over time. By establishing governance policies, managing the content lifecycle, updating metadata and taxonomy, and monitoring usage, you can keep your DAM aligned with organizational goals. Continuous training, user feedback, and scalability planning ensure the DAM remains valuable, adaptable, and capable of supporting growing demands. With these best practices, your DAM can evolve into a long-term asset that drives productivity, collaboration, and brand consistency.

In the next chapter, we'll look toward the future of DAM and explore emerging trends, such as AI-driven content personalization and advanced integrations, to help you prepare for what's next in digital asset management.

Part 5:
Best Practices for Ongoing Usage and Optimization

Implementing a Digital Asset Management (DAM) system is a significant investment, but maintaining its value requires an ongoing commitment to strategy, alignment, and adaptability. Part 5 explores the keys to achieving long-term success with your DAM, focusing on sustainable management practices, maximizing ROI, and ensuring continuous alignment with organizational goals.

In this section, we'll discuss how to monitor and measure DAM performance, refine processes as your organization grows, and adapt to emerging technologies and evolving user needs. By adopting a forward-thinking approach to DAM management, your organization can leverage its full potential, ensuring that the system remains an integral part of efficient workflows, brand consistency, and cross-departmental collaboration. Through proactive strategies and regular evaluations, your DAM can deliver lasting value and support your organization's digital asset needs well into the future.

Chapter 13: Establishing DAM Governance and Usage Guidelines

Defining governance roles, asset lifecycle management, and usage policies and tips on how to enforce brand guidelines and ensure data security.

TL;DR

The future of DAM is driven by emerging technologies that enhance functionality and adaptability. AI-driven personalization and predictive analytics enable targeted content delivery and data-informed content strategy. Enhanced integrations with martech tools streamline workflows, while voice and visual search improve asset discoverability. Blockchain offers secure rights management, tracking asset usage with transparency. Advanced automation allows dynamic content delivery and automated formatting, saving time and ensuring consistency. AI also supports DAM maintenance by automating tagging, predictive upkeep, and user behavior analysis, keeping the DAM organized and efficient as it scales with your organization's needs.

As the digital landscape evolves, so does the potential for Digital Asset Management (DAM) systems to support more sophisticated, data-driven marketing and content strategies. Emerging technologies, particularly in artificial intelligence (AI), automation, and personalization, are shaping the future of DAM, offering new ways to manage, optimize, and leverage digital assets. In this chapter, we'll explore key trends and technologies that are driving the next generation of DAM systems, from AI-driven content personalization to advanced integrations and predictive analytics. Understanding these trends can help your organization prepare to enhance your DAM's capabilities, staying ahead of the curve and maximizing the value of your digital assets.

13.1 AI-Driven Personalization and Content Recommendations

One of the most transformative trends in DAM is the rise of AI-driven personalization, which uses machine learning to tailor content recommendations based on audience behavior and preferences. This enables marketers to deliver more targeted, relevant experiences across channels, increasing engagement and conversion rates.

- **Audience Segmentation**: AI can analyze user behavior and segment audiences based on characteristics like location, engagement level, and purchase history. DAMs can then recommend assets for each segment, optimizing content for different demographics.
- **Content Recommendations**: AI-driven recommendations surface assets that are likely to perform well based on historical data, campaign goals, or content themes. This feature enables marketers to choose high-performing visuals that resonate with specific audiences.
- **Dynamic Content Delivery**: Some DAMs integrate with personalization engines to deliver dynamic content in real-time. For example, a DAM could automatically adjust visuals on a website based on a visitor's past interactions, creating a more personalized experience.

Example: AI-Driven Personalization in E-Commerce

An e-commerce brand uses AI-powered segmentation in their DAM to tailor product visuals for different customer segments. Returning customers see personalized product recommendations, while new visitors are shown popular items, enhancing relevance and boosting conversions.

13.2 Predictive Analytics for Content Strategy and Planning

Predictive analytics is transforming DAM by providing insights into which assets are likely to succeed based on past performance and market trends. Predictive capabilities enable marketing teams to make data-driven decisions about content creation, campaign planning, and asset optimization.

- **Asset Performance Prediction**: Predictive analytics can forecast which assets will likely perform well based on past campaigns, enabling teams to prioritize high-impact content and reduce wasted resources.
- **Campaign Planning Insights**: DAM systems equipped with predictive tools can help marketers anticipate content needs for upcoming campaigns. By analyzing trends, predictive analytics offer insights into seasonality and audience preferences.
- **Data-Driven Content Creation**: Predictive insights help guide content development by identifying themes, visuals, or messaging that resonates with target audiences. This enables creative teams to align assets with projected audience interests.

Example: Predictive Analytics in a B2B Software Company

A B2B software company uses predictive analytics in their DAM to assess which types of case studies and whitepapers are most effective at each stage of the sales funnel. By focusing on content that performs well with prospects, they can drive engagement and optimize resource allocation.

13.3 Enhanced Integrations with Martech Ecosystems

DAM systems are increasingly becoming part of integrated martech ecosystems, connecting seamlessly with other marketing and sales tools to streamline asset use across channels. Enhanced integrations enable faster, more efficient workflows, making it easier for teams to distribute assets and track content performance.

- **CMS and CRM Integrations**: DAMs that integrate with content management systems (CMS) and customer relationship management (CRM) platforms enable marketers to access assets directly within these tools. This seamless access supports consistent brand messaging across websites, emails, and customer interactions.
- **Social Media and Ad Platforms**: Integrating DAM with social media scheduling tools and ad platforms allows marketers to push

assets directly to campaigns, track performance, and update visuals across channels without leaving the DAM.
- **Project Management and Collaboration Tools**: DAMs connected to project management tools (like Asana or Trello) support streamlined workflows by linking assets directly to projects, facilitating better task tracking and collaboration.

Example: Martech Integration for a Global Consumer Brand

A global consumer brand integrates its DAM with its CMS and social media scheduling tools. Marketers access approved assets directly in these platforms, reducing time spent transferring files and ensuring brand consistency across web, email, and social media.

13.4 Voice and Visual Search Capabilities

Voice and visual search are emerging technologies that can enhance DAM usability by making asset discovery faster and more intuitive. These capabilities allow users to locate assets based on spoken commands or similar visual elements, expanding search beyond traditional keywords and tags.

- **Voice Search**: Voice-activated search allows users to search for assets by speaking, a feature that can improve usability and accessibility. This is particularly helpful for users multitasking or accessing the DAM on mobile devices.

- **Visual Search and Similarity Matching**: Visual search uses AI to identify and surface assets with similar visual characteristics, such as color, layout, or subject matter. This helps users find visually consistent assets for campaigns, especially useful for creatives managing large asset libraries.
- **Image Recognition for Tagging**: AI-driven image recognition can automatically tag assets based on visual elements, making it easier to locate content even if specific keywords are missing.

Example: Visual Search for a Travel Company

A travel company uses visual search to find similar images for campaign consistency. By selecting a "beach" photo, they can pull up other beach-related visuals, ensuring a cohesive look across their ads, social media, and website content.

13.5 Blockchain for Digital Rights Management

Blockchain technology offers a secure, transparent way to manage digital rights and asset ownership, making it easier to track asset usage and prevent unauthorized distribution. While still emerging in DAM, blockchain has the potential to transform rights management by creating verifiable, immutable records.

- **Smart Contracts for Licensing**: Blockchain can facilitate smart contracts that automatically enforce licensing terms. For example,

a DAM could restrict asset access based on license agreements stored on a blockchain, preventing unauthorized use.
- **Ownership Verification**: Blockchain records provide an unalterable history of asset ownership, allowing organizations to track asset origin, licensing, and usage. This is especially valuable for managing high-value assets, like exclusive photography or artwork.
- **Transparency in Asset Usage**: Blockchain can help organizations maintain transparency by providing an audit trail of how, when, and by whom each asset is used. This visibility reduces compliance risks and enhances trust with asset contributors.

Example: Blockchain for Rights Management in Media

A media company uses blockchain to manage rights for video content. Smart contracts restrict video usage to specific channels, with the blockchain ledger tracking all views and downloads, ensuring compliance with licensing agreements.

13.6 Advanced Content Automation and Dynamic Delivery

Automation is expanding within DAM, allowing for more dynamic asset delivery and content adaptation across channels. Dynamic content adapts in real-time based on audience data, while automation tools streamline the creation and distribution of personalized visuals.

- **Automated Content Resizing and Formatting**: Automated resizing tools allow users to download assets in preset formats, optimizing content for different platforms (e.g., resizing for Instagram vs. LinkedIn) without manual editing.
- **Personalized Dynamic Delivery**: Dynamic content delivery uses audience data to adapt visuals in real-time, ensuring the right content reaches the right person at the right moment. This is especially valuable for digital advertising, where targeting can drive engagement.
- **Automated Workflow Triggers**: Automated workflows can trigger actions based on user behavior, such as notifying the marketing team when an asset reaches a download threshold or alerting legal when a license is about to expire.

Example: Automated Content Delivery for a Retail Brand

A retail brand's DAM system uses automation to resize product images based on where they'll be used. For example, images downloaded for social media are automatically sized for the platform's requirements, saving time and maintaining quality.

13.7 The Role of AI in DAM Maintenance and Optimization

As DAM systems become more complex, AI is playing a key role in maintaining organization, optimizing performance, and enhancing user experience. AI tools can streamline maintenance tasks, reduce administrative workload, and keep the DAM aligned with organizational needs.

- **Automated Metadata Tagging**: AI-driven metadata tagging helps keep the DAM organized by automatically tagging new assets. This reduces the need for manual tagging and ensures that assets remain easy to locate as the library grows.
- **Predictive Maintenance**: AI can detect patterns in asset usage or metadata inconsistencies, alerting administrators to potential issues. Predictive maintenance helps keep the DAM running smoothly and minimizes downtime.
- **User Behavior Analysis**: By analyzing user activity, AI can suggest improvements to the DAM's configuration or highlight features that could enhance the user experience, such as popular search filters or shortcut options.

Example: AI-Assisted Maintenance for a Marketing Agency

A marketing agency's DAM uses AI to monitor asset usage and recommend updates to popular search filters. By automating these adjustments, the agency ensures that assets remain easy to find, and users get a more streamlined experience.

Conclusion

The future of DAM is defined by advancements in AI, automation, blockchain, and integrations that enhance functionality, security, and user experience. From personalized content recommendations and predictive analytics to seamless integrations and dynamic delivery, these trends will transform how organizations manage and leverage digital assets. As you plan for the future of your DAM, consider how these emerging technologies can support your long-term goals, creating a DAM that adapts to change, enhances productivity, and provides strategic value.

In the final chapter, we'll summarize key takeaways from this guide and provide actionable steps to ensure your DAM continues to serve as a valuable asset for your organization.

Chapter 14: Integrating DAM with Your Marketing Technology Stack

Discussing key integrations to optimize workflows: CMS, CRM, project management, and creative tools as well as benefits of connected systems for seamless asset use and tracking.

TL;DR

Regular evaluation of DAM effectiveness ensures it continues to deliver value and meet user needs. Start by setting clear goals aligned with organizational priorities. Track key performance metrics such as search efficiency, asset reuse, and workflow speed, and calculate ROI based on time savings and cost reductions. Gather user feedback through surveys and focus groups to capture qualitative insights, and assess how well the DAM supports goals like brand consistency and compliance. Use findings to identify areas for improvement, refine metadata, optimize workflows, and provide additional training. Establish an ongoing evaluation process to keep the DAM adaptable and valuable over time.

To ensure that your DAM continues to deliver value, it's essential to evaluate its effectiveness regularly. A thorough evaluation allows you to understand how well the DAM is meeting user needs, whether it's supporting business goals, and where improvements can be made. By tracking key metrics, gathering user feedback, and assessing overall alignment with organizational objectives, you can identify areas for optimization and keep your DAM functioning at peak performance. In this chapter, we'll discuss evaluating DAM effectiveness through performance metrics, ROI calculations, user satisfaction surveys, and alignment with strategic goals.

14.1 Setting Clear Evaluation Goals

Before diving into specific metrics, it's important to define clear evaluation goals that align with your organization's priorities. Establishing these goals ensures that you focus on the areas of DAM performance that matter most.

- **Identify Key Performance Areas**: Decide which aspects of DAM performance are most important, such as user satisfaction, asset accessibility, or workflow efficiency.
- **Align with Organizational Objectives**: Ensure that DAM evaluation goals are aligned with broader business objectives, such as improving campaign speed, enhancing brand consistency, or increasing productivity.
- **Define Success Criteria**: Set criteria for what successful DAM performance looks like. For instance, you might aim for a specific increase in asset reuse, faster search times, or high user satisfaction scores.

Example: Evaluation Goals for a B2B SaaS Company

A B2B SaaS company sets evaluation goals focused on improving asset accessibility and reducing time spent on asset searches. Their success criteria include increasing search efficiency by 20% and achieving an 80% user satisfaction score for ease of access.

14.2 Tracking Key Performance Metrics

Measuring the right metrics is crucial for a thorough evaluation. These metrics provide concrete data that reveal how effectively the DAM is supporting users and helping the organization achieve its goals.

- **Search Efficiency**: Track how long users spend searching for assets and the number of searches required to find the right asset. Reduced search times indicate an organized and efficient DAM.
- **Asset Reuse Rate**: Monitor how frequently assets are reused across campaigns or departments. A higher reuse rate reflects effective asset discoverability and utilization.
- **Download and Access Frequency**: Measure the frequency with which assets are accessed and downloaded. High usage rates often indicate valuable, high-demand assets and can guide future content creation.
- **Workflow Completion Time**: Evaluate the time required to complete key workflows, such as approvals or asset uploads. Efficient workflows demonstrate a well-configured DAM that supports fast, seamless collaboration.

Example: Tracking Metrics for a Retail Brand

A retail brand tracks asset reuse rates, noting that product images are frequently reused across social media and email campaigns. This metric highlights the DAM's role in supporting consistent branding and reducing content production time.

14.3 Calculating DAM ROI

Calculating the return on investment (ROI) of your DAM system helps justify its value to stakeholders and demonstrates how it contributes to the organization's bottom line. DAM ROI can be measured by analyzing productivity gains, cost savings, and time efficiency.

- **Time Savings**: Quantify the time saved by users when searching for assets, organizing content, or navigating workflows. Multiply this time savings by average employee hourly rates to estimate productivity gains.
- **Reduction in Redundant Content Creation**: Measure the cost savings from reducing duplicate asset creation. By reusing existing assets, teams can save on production costs and time, contributing to overall ROI.
- **Improved Speed to Market**: Calculate how much faster campaigns can be launched due to efficient asset management. Faster time-to-market often leads to increased revenue potential and enhanced competitiveness.

Example: Calculating ROI for a Financial Services Firm

A financial services firm calculates DAM ROI by measuring time savings from faster asset searches and reduced duplication of materials. They find that the DAM saves the company an estimated $100,000 annually in reduced production costs and increased productivity.

14.4 Gathering User Feedback for Qualitative Insights

Quantitative metrics are valuable, but they don't capture the full user experience. Gathering feedback from users provides qualitative insights that reveal satisfaction levels, ease of use, and potential areas for improvement.

- **Conduct User Surveys**: Use surveys to collect feedback on DAM usability, favorite features, and challenges. Regular surveys help keep a pulse on user satisfaction and can highlight specific needs or frustrations.
- **Hold Focus Groups**: Focus groups allow you to dive deeper into user experiences, gathering detailed insights and identifying common themes. Focus groups work well for discussing new feature needs or exploring workflow challenges.
- **Monitor Support Requests**: Review support tickets and requests to identify recurring issues or user pain points. High-frequency issues can point to usability gaps or training needs.

Example: User Feedback for a Media Company

A media company conducts quarterly DAM surveys, asking users to rate ease of access and search functionality. Feedback reveals that users find the tagging system overly complex, prompting a review of metadata fields to streamline search and tagging processes.

14.5 Assessing Alignment with Organizational Goals

Evaluating how well your DAM aligns with organizational goals helps ensure it remains a strategic asset. Consider how effectively the DAM supports initiatives like brand consistency, compliance, and cross-departmental collaboration.

- **Brand Consistency**: Evaluate how well the DAM supports brand consistency by tracking asset usage and identifying assets that align with brand guidelines. Consistent asset use contributes to a cohesive brand image.
- **Regulatory Compliance**: Assess whether the DAM's rights management and permissions settings effectively support compliance requirements, especially if your organization operates in a regulated industry.
- **Cross-Departmental Collaboration**: Analyze how the DAM facilitates collaboration across teams. High collaboration levels often indicate a DAM that's easy to use and accessible to multiple departments, enhancing productivity and alignment.

Example: Organizational Alignment for a Pharmaceutical Company

A pharmaceutical company reviews its DAM's role in supporting compliance by assessing permissions and usage tracking. They find that the DAM's rights management features significantly reduce the risk of unauthorized content usage, strengthening regulatory compliance.

14.6 Identifying Areas for Improvement

Through evaluating metrics, gathering feedback, and assessing goal alignment, you'll uncover areas where the DAM could be optimized. Identifying these improvement areas allows you to make targeted changes that enhance the DAM's value and functionality.

- **Improve Metadata and Taxonomy**: If search efficiency is low, consider refining metadata and taxonomy to make assets easier to locate. Simplified tags or expanded categories can improve asset discoverability.
- **Enhance User Training**: If users report difficulty navigating the DAM, additional training or refresher sessions can boost confidence and usability. Updated training materials or video tutorials can address recurring issues.
- **Optimize Workflows**: Streamline workflows by reducing unnecessary approval steps or simplifying task assignments. Faster workflows improve user satisfaction and reduce delays in asset delivery.

Example: Optimizing a DAM for a Non-Profit

A non-profit organization reviews DAM feedback and finds that users struggle with search filters. They refine metadata categories to improve search accuracy and provide additional training, increasing user satisfaction and search efficiency.

14.7 Creating an Ongoing Evaluation Process

Evaluating DAM effectiveness should be an ongoing process. Regular evaluations allow you to keep the system aligned with user needs and organizational goals as they evolve over time.

- **Set a Regular Evaluation Schedule**: Establish a schedule for quarterly or biannual DAM evaluations, reviewing performance metrics, feedback, and ROI calculations.
- **Incorporate Feedback Loops**: Regularly solicit feedback from users to capture evolving needs and identify emerging pain points. Use this feedback to inform updates or optimizations.
- **Document Improvements**: Keep a record of changes made to the DAM based on evaluations, tracking how these adjustments impact user satisfaction and performance. Documenting improvements demonstrates continuous progress and supports accountability.

Example: Ongoing Evaluation for a Consumer Brand

A consumer brand conducts quarterly DAM reviews, using a consistent set of metrics and surveys to track changes in asset usage and user satisfaction. By addressing feedback promptly, they keep the DAM relevant and user-friendly, supporting efficient campaign execution.

Conclusion

Evaluating DAM effectiveness involves setting clear goals, tracking performance metrics, calculating ROI, gathering user feedback, and aligning with organizational objectives. By identifying improvement areas and establishing a regular evaluation process, you can ensure that the DAM continues to meet user needs, support business goals, and deliver lasting value. An ongoing evaluation approach allows your DAM to evolve with your organization, staying relevant, efficient, and impactful.

In the next chapter, we'll discuss how to scale your DAM to accommodate growth, adapt to new asset types, and support expanding teams, ensuring it remains a versatile and sustainable tool for the future.

Chapter 15: Measuring Success and Continuously Optimizing Your DAM

Exploring KPIs to monitor DAM performance, like asset usage, time savings, and user satisfaction and techniques to gather feedback, iterate on workflows, and update asset categorization as needs evolve.

TL;DR

Scaling a DAM system to support growth requires planning for expanded storage, adapting metadata and taxonomy, and optimizing performance as asset volumes increase. Implement archiving policies, add relevant metadata fields,

and configure role-based workflows to support larger teams and cross-functional use. Strengthen security with role-based access control and multi-factor authentication to protect sensitive content as users and departments expand. Prepare for future integrations with open APIs and stay informed on emerging DAM technologies. By proactively managing these areas, you ensure your DAM remains effective, adaptable, and valuable as your organization grows.

As organizations grow, so do the demands placed on their DAM systems. New teams, expanded asset libraries, and evolving content needs require a DAM that can adapt and scale. Successfully scaling a DAM involves planning for increased asset volume, accommodating diverse user needs, expanding metadata and taxonomy structures, and ensuring the system remains fast and user-friendly. This chapter covers strategies to scale your DAM effectively, including planning for storage growth, adapting workflows, optimizing system performance, and managing cross-functional use cases. By proactively preparing for growth, you can ensure that your DAM continues to support your organization's evolving needs without sacrificing efficiency or usability.

15.1 Planning for Increased Storage Capacity

As your asset library grows, so does the need for storage. Planning for future storage needs ensures that your DAM can support expanding content without performance issues, such as slow load times or search lags.

- **Evaluate Storage Options**: Review your DAM's storage options and scalability features. Some DAMs offer flexible storage plans that allow you to increase capacity as needed, while others may require a specific upgrade.
- **Implement Archiving Policies**: To optimize storage, implement archiving policies that move outdated or less frequently used assets to secondary storage. Archived assets remain accessible without taking up primary storage space.
- **Monitor Storage Usage**: Regularly monitor your DAM's storage usage and set usage thresholds. Proactive monitoring allows you to upgrade storage capacity before reaching critical levels, preventing disruptions.

Example: Storage Management for a Media Company

A media company with a rapidly growing video library monitors storage usage closely and archives older content to manage capacity. By keeping the primary storage organized, they ensure quick access to active assets without impacting system speed.

15.2 Expanding Metadata and Taxonomy Structures

As new assets, campaigns, and departments are added to the DAM, your metadata and taxonomy structures may need to expand to accommodate these changes. Adapting metadata and taxonomy makes it easier for users to locate assets as the library grows.

- **Add New Metadata Fields**: If your organization is producing new types of content or targeting new markets, consider adding relevant metadata fields. For example, adding a "campaign type" field can help organize assets for different marketing initiatives.
- **Create Subcategories for Large Asset Groups**: As asset categories grow, introduce subcategories to keep the taxonomy organized. This structure prevents overcrowding in top-level categories and enhances search accuracy.
- **Update Naming Conventions**: Establish naming conventions that accommodate new assets, teams, or product lines. Consistent naming improves discoverability and prevents confusion as the DAM grows.

Example: Expanding Taxonomy for a Global Retailer

A global retailer expands its DAM's taxonomy by adding regional subcategories to accommodate assets for different markets. The additional structure enables teams in various regions to quickly locate relevant content, supporting localized campaigns.

15.3 Optimizing DAM Performance for Large Libraries

A growing asset library can impact DAM performance if not properly managed. Optimizing DAM performance helps ensure that users can search, access, and download assets without delays, even as the library expands.

- **Use AI-Driven Search Optimization**: Some DAMs offer AI-powered search features that can help speed up searches in large libraries by prioritizing relevant results and auto-suggesting terms.
- **Enable Caching and Pre-Loading for Popular Assets**: Frequently accessed assets can be preloaded or cached to reduce load times. This technique improves performance by minimizing load times for high-traffic assets.
- **Regularly Clean Up and Archive**: Removing duplicates, outdated assets, and unnecessary files reduces database size and improves search speed. Implement a regular cleanup schedule to keep the library streamlined.

Example: Performance Optimization for an E-Commerce Brand

An e-commerce brand with thousands of product images implements AI-driven search optimization to speed up asset retrieval. They also cache high-demand assets to ensure that product images load quickly, improving user experience and productivity.

15.4 Adapting Workflows to Support Larger Teams

As your organization scales, so does the need for efficient, adaptable workflows that support a growing number of users. Configuring workflows that accommodate large teams ensures that tasks remain streamlined, deadlines are met, and collaboration flows smoothly.

- **Set Up Role-Based Workflows**: With more users, role-based workflows become essential. Assign specific roles and permissions based on department needs, ensuring users only see workflows relevant to their tasks.
- **Automate Notifications for Key Tasks**: Automate notifications for tasks like approvals, uploads, or tagging to keep everyone informed without manual reminders. Automated alerts help reduce communication bottlenecks and keep workflows moving.
- **Create Department-Specific Workflows**: As the DAM's user base expands, consider creating department-specific workflows tailored to different teams, such as marketing, creative, or legal. Customized workflows improve efficiency and ensure tasks are relevant to each team's needs.

Example: Workflow Customization for a Financial Services Firm

A financial services firm configures department-specific workflows in their DAM, creating separate approval processes for marketing, compliance, and product teams. This approach streamlines cross-departmental collaboration while maintaining compliance standards.

15.5 Managing Cross-Functional Use Cases

When multiple departments use the DAM, cross-functional needs must be managed effectively to ensure all users can find and access the assets they need. Managing these use cases supports collaboration and prevents conflicts over asset usage or permissions.

- **Define Access Levels for Each Department**: Set clear access levels for each department based on their content needs. For instance, marketing may need access to all campaign assets, while sales may only need access to select product images.
- **Create Shared Libraries for High-Use Assets**: Establish shared folders for assets commonly used across departments, such as logos or brand templates. Shared libraries improve access and maintain consistency.
- **Hold Cross-Departmental Training**: Provide training sessions that cover best practices for cross-functional use. This helps users understand how to navigate the DAM, follow naming conventions, and respect other departments' permissions.

Example: Cross-Functional Asset Management for a University

A university's DAM supports marketing, admissions, and alumni relations. By creating shared libraries for high-use assets like campus photos and event banners, each department can access resources without duplicating files or conflicting over permissions.

15.6 Ensuring Security and Compliance as the DAM Scales

As the DAM grows, so does the importance of robust security and compliance protocols, especially if new departments or external partners begin using the system. Effective security measures protect sensitive content and maintain regulatory compliance.

- **Expand Role-Based Access Control**: As the user base grows, configure detailed role-based access control (RBAC) settings to restrict access to sensitive or proprietary content. RBAC ensures that each user can only access the assets relevant to their role.
- **Monitor Compliance Requirements**: If your organization is subject to regulatory standards, regularly audit the DAM to ensure it continues to comply with requirements, such as GDPR, CCPA, or industry-specific regulations.
- **Implement Multi-Factor Authentication (MFA)**: Add an extra layer of security by enabling MFA, especially if external contractors or third parties have access to the DAM. MFA reduces the risk of unauthorized access and strengthens data protection.

Example: Security Protocols for a Healthcare Organization

A healthcare organization uses RBAC and multi-factor authentication to protect patient-related assets and ensure compliance with HIPAA. Regular audits help maintain compliance, even as the DAM's user base and asset library expand.

15.7 Planning for Future Integrations and Technological Advancements

Scalability isn't only about handling more assets and users; it's also about preparing for future integrations and new technologies. Planning for these advancements ensures that your DAM remains adaptable and continues to deliver value as new tools and capabilities become available.

- **Evaluate Integration Options**: Identify platforms that could integrate with your DAM in the future, such as CRM, project management, or AI-driven personalization tools. Future-ready DAMs with open APIs make integration easier as your martech stack evolves.
- **Stay Informed on Emerging Technologies**: Keep track of emerging DAM technologies, such as AI-driven tagging or blockchain-based rights management. Understanding these trends will help you identify new features that could enhance the DAM.
- **Regularly Reassess Your DAM's Scalability**: Conduct periodic reviews to ensure the DAM can support future needs, such as larger asset volumes or advanced features. This proactive approach keeps the DAM aligned with the organization's growth trajectory.

Example: Future-Ready Planning for a Tech Start-Up

A tech start-up anticipates rapid growth and plans for future integrations with their CRM and AI tools for content personalization. They choose a DAM with an open API, allowing easy integration with new platforms as their marketing technology stack expands.

Conclusion

Scaling a DAM effectively involves planning for storage, expanding metadata and taxonomy, optimizing performance, and managing cross-functional use. By adapting workflows, strengthening security, and planning for future integrations, you can ensure that the DAM continues to meet your organization's needs as it grows. With a proactive approach to scalability, your DAM can remain a reliable and versatile tool that drives productivity, supports collaboration, and evolves alongside your business.

In the next chapter, we'll summarize the key takeaways from this guide and outline actionable steps for creating a sustainable, high-impact DAM strategy.

Part 6: Future-Proofing Your DAM Investment

Implementing a Digital Asset Management (DAM) system is a significant investment, but maintaining its value requires an ongoing commitment to strategy, alignment, and adaptability. Part 5 explores the keys to achieving long-term success with your DAM, focusing on sustainable management practices, maximizing ROI, and ensuring continuous alignment with organizational goals.

In this final section, we'll discuss how to monitor and measure DAM performance, refine processes as your organization grows, and adapt to emerging technologies and evolving user needs. By adopting a forward-thinking approach to DAM management, your organization can leverage its full potential, ensuring that the system remains an integral part of efficient workflows, brand consistency, and cross-departmental collaboration. Through proactive strategies and regular evaluations, your DAM can deliver lasting value and support your organization's digital asset needs well into the future.

Chapter 16: Keeping Up with DAM Trends and Innovations

Discussing upcoming trends: AI advancements, augmented reality assets, and personalized content automation.

TL;DR

Building a sustainable DAM strategy involves establishing governance, fostering user engagement, planning for growth, and committing to continuous improvement. Define clear roles and guidelines to maintain organization and compliance, encourage user feedback to optimize functionality, and regularly review storage and workflows to support scalability. Align the DAM with organizational goals like brand consistency and regulatory compliance, and stay informed on emerging technologies to keep the DAM adaptable. With this proactive approach, your DAM will remain a valuable, strategic resource that grows alongside your organization.

A Digital Asset Management (DAM) system is a powerful tool for organizing, managing, and distributing digital assets, but its true potential is realized through a long-term strategy that ensures it remains aligned with organizational goals. Building a sustainable DAM strategy requires a proactive approach to governance, regular evaluations, and a commitment to ongoing optimization and user support. In this chapter, we'll cover the key components of a sustainable DAM strategy, including establishing governance frameworks, fostering user engagement, planning for future growth, and setting up systems for continuous improvement. By following these best practices, your DAM can remain a valuable, adaptable resource that supports efficient workflows, collaboration, and brand consistency for years to come.

16.1 Establishing a Strong Governance Framework

Governance is the backbone of a sustainable DAM strategy. A clear governance framework defines how the DAM will be managed, who is responsible for specific tasks, and how decisions are made to ensure consistency and compliance.

- **Define Roles and Responsibilities**: Assign specific roles, such as DAM administrator, content curators, and department leads, to manage and maintain the DAM. Clearly defining roles reduces ambiguity and ensures accountability.
- **Develop DAM Guidelines and Policies**: Establish guidelines for asset naming conventions, metadata standards, and usage rights. These policies help maintain consistency and make it easy for users to locate and manage assets.

- **Implement an Approval Process for Asset Additions**: Create a workflow for approving new assets before they are added to the DAM. This ensures only high-quality, relevant content enters the system, preserving organization and usability.

Example: Governance for a Consumer Goods Company

A consumer goods company assigns a DAM administrator to oversee system management, while each department designates content curators responsible for asset quality and organization. Guidelines for metadata, naming conventions, and asset rights help keep the DAM consistent and compliant.

16.2 Fostering User Engagement and Adoption

An effective DAM strategy requires strong user engagement and adoption. Encouraging users to incorporate the DAM into their daily workflows and promoting consistent use across departments ensures that the system remains a central resource.

- **Provide Ongoing Training and Support**: Offer regular training sessions, especially when new features are introduced or workflows change. Ensure users have access to resources like user guides and a helpdesk for support.
- **Encourage User Contributions and Feedback**: Involve users in the DAM's evolution by encouraging feedback on features,

workflows, and potential improvements. User feedback can reveal insights that help optimize the system.
- **Recognize Power Users and Early Adopters**: Highlight and reward users who actively engage with the DAM, as they can serve as champions and provide peer support. Recognition programs promote adoption and motivate others to use the DAM effectively.

Example: Engagement Strategy for a Marketing Team

A marketing team hosts monthly DAM workshops and recognizes top users in internal newsletters, fostering a positive culture of DAM engagement. Regular feedback sessions allow team members to suggest improvements, keeping the DAM aligned with user needs.

16.3 Planning for Future Growth and Scalability

A sustainable DAM strategy includes plans for future growth, ensuring that the system can adapt as your organization and asset library expand. Preparing for scalability prevents disruptions and allows the DAM to accommodate new content, users, and features.

- **Regularly Assess Storage Needs**: As the asset library grows, monitor storage usage and plan for capacity increases. Proactively expanding storage helps avoid slowdowns and ensures assets are accessible.
- **Anticipate New Asset Types**: Be prepared to add metadata fields and taxonomy categories as new types of content emerge, such as

video, 3D models, or interactive assets. Flexibility in metadata and taxonomy supports evolving needs.
- **Review and Update Workflows**: As the DAM's user base grows, workflows may need to be adjusted to handle higher volumes of assets and approvals. Periodic workflow reviews ensure that processes remain efficient as team size and responsibilities expand.

Example: Growth Planning for an E-Commerce Brand

An e-commerce brand reviews storage quarterly to accommodate seasonal content growth. They expand taxonomy to include metadata for new product categories, supporting the brand's growing inventory and allowing users to easily locate relevant assets.

16.4 Implementing Continuous Improvement Practices

A sustainable DAM strategy involves ongoing evaluation and optimization. Establishing processes for continuous improvement allows the DAM to stay aligned with user needs and evolving business goals.

- **Set Regular Evaluation Intervals**: Schedule quarterly or biannual DAM evaluations to assess performance, gather user feedback, and identify areas for improvement. Regular assessments keep the system optimized.
- **Monitor Key Metrics and ROI**: Track metrics like search efficiency, asset usage, and workflow completion times to evaluate

DAM performance. Calculating ROI helps demonstrate the DAM's value and identify cost-saving opportunities.
- **Update the DAM Based on Feedback and Trends**: Use feedback and insights from evaluations to make iterative updates. This might include adding new metadata fields, refining workflows, or implementing new features based on industry trends.

Example: Continuous Improvement for a Healthcare Organization

A healthcare organization conducts semiannual DAM evaluations and solicits feedback from users on asset organization and metadata accuracy. By incorporating feedback into system updates, they ensure the DAM meets compliance standards and remains user-friendly.

16.5 Maintaining Alignment with Organizational Goals

A sustainable DAM strategy ensures that the system continues to support broader organizational goals, such as brand consistency, compliance, and collaboration across teams. Aligning the DAM with these objectives maximizes its strategic impact.

- **Review Organizational Objectives Regularly**: As company goals evolve, ensure the DAM remains aligned by revisiting objectives periodically. For instance, if brand consistency becomes a focus, consider optimizing metadata for brand guidelines.

- **Align DAM Policies with Compliance Requirements**: If your organization operates in a regulated industry, regularly audit DAM settings to ensure compliance with standards like GDPR, CCPA, or HIPAA.
- **Support Cross-Functional Use Cases**: As more departments use the DAM, work to align workflows and permissions with their specific needs. Facilitating cross-functional collaboration ensures that the DAM serves as a centralized resource for all users.

Example: Goal Alignment for a Financial Services Firm

A financial services firm aligns its DAM with regulatory requirements by conducting annual compliance audits. They also update metadata fields to ensure consistent use of approved terminology, supporting brand integrity and compliance.

16.6 Adopting a Forward-Looking Approach to DAM Technology

Technology continues to evolve, and a sustainable DAM strategy involves staying informed about new advancements. By adopting a forward-looking approach, you can prepare to implement innovative features that add value to the DAM over time.

- **Monitor Emerging Trends and Technologies**: Stay up-to-date with DAM industry developments, such as AI-driven search, automated tagging, or blockchain for rights management.

Understanding trends allows you to proactively consider new features.
- **Plan for Future Integrations**: Identify tools that might integrate with your DAM in the future, such as AI personalization engines or advanced analytics platforms. Selecting a DAM with open APIs facilitates seamless integrations down the line.
- **Create a DAM Innovation Roadmap**: Outline a long-term plan for DAM improvements and new feature implementation. Having a roadmap helps prioritize enhancements that align with your organization's strategic objectives.

Example: Future-Ready DAM Strategy for a Tech Start-Up

A tech start-up keeps an innovation roadmap for their DAM, planning future integrations with their CRM and AI-powered recommendation engine. This approach ensures the DAM continues to support the start-up's growth and content personalization needs.

Conclusion

Creating a sustainable DAM strategy involves establishing strong governance, fostering user engagement, preparing for growth, and committing to continuous improvement. By aligning the DAM with organizational goals, monitoring for future technological advancements, and proactively adapting to change, you ensure that your DAM remains a valuable, strategic asset over time. A sustainable DAM strategy supports efficient workflows, strengthens brand consistency, and fosters cross-functional collaboration, empowering your team to make the most of digital assets today and into the future.

In the next chapter, we'll roffer actionable steps to solidify your DAM strategy, ensuring long-term success.

Chapter 17: Preparing for the Future of Content and DAM

Discussing how DAM will evolve to support multi-channel marketing, dynamic personalization, and real-time content creation.

TL;DR

The future of DAM will support multi-channel marketing, dynamic personalization, and real-time content creation. Advanced DAM systems will enable seamless asset adaptation for different platforms, maintain consistency across channels, and allow for automated resizing and variant creation. Integrated with AI and customer data

platforms, future DAMs will facilitate personalized content delivery and real-time customization based on user data. DAMs will also enhance real-time workflows with collaborative tools, automated approvals, and instant distribution across channels. As emerging technologies like AR, VR, and blockchain influence content, DAMs will adapt to store and manage these new formats, future-proofing organizations for evolving marketing strategies.

As digital marketing becomes increasingly dynamic and data-driven, the demands on Digital Asset Management (DAM) systems continue to evolve. To stay competitive, organizations need a DAM that can support multi-channel marketing, enable dynamic personalization, and facilitate real-time content creation and distribution. The future of DAM is centered on adaptability, automation, and integration, helping marketers deliver consistent, personalized experiences at scale across multiple platforms. In this chapter, we'll explore how DAM systems are evolving to meet these new challenges and how your organization can prepare to leverage DAM for future-focused marketing strategies.

17.1 Supporting Multi-Channel Marketing

In today's digital landscape, consumers interact with brands across numerous channels—from websites and social media to email and in-store displays. Multi-channel marketing relies on delivering a seamless, consistent experience across each touchpoint, and DAM plays a vital role in enabling this by centralizing assets and ensuring they are accessible, adaptable, and aligned with brand guidelines.

- **Centralized Access to Multi-Channel Assets**: Future DAMs will enhance centralized access to assets across platforms, making it easier for teams to locate and deploy content suited to specific channels. Advanced metadata and tagging allow assets to be categorized by platform requirements, such as aspect ratio or resolution, streamlining the adaptation process.
- **Channel-Specific Variants and Adaptations**: DAMs are evolving to support automated resizing, reformatting, and even content variant creation, allowing assets to be quickly adapted for different platforms without manual intervention. With one-click adjustments, a single asset can be optimized for use on a website, social media, or a mobile app.
- **Consistency Across Channels**: A DAM that integrates seamlessly with other marketing technologies (e.g., CMS, CRM, social media management tools) enables consistent asset deployment across channels. By pulling assets directly from the DAM, marketers ensure that content is always brand-compliant, up-to-date, and aligned with campaign messaging.

Example: Multi-Channel Asset Management for a Retail Brand

A retail brand uses a DAM with channel-specific metadata and one-click resizing to prepare product images for web, email, and social media channels. This allows their marketing team to deploy campaign assets efficiently while maintaining a consistent look and feel across all platforms.

17.2 Enabling Dynamic Personalization and Customization

Personalization is increasingly central to marketing strategies, with consumers expecting content tailored to their preferences, behaviors, and needs. DAM systems are evolving to support dynamic content personalization by integrating with AI and customer data platforms (CDPs) to enable real-time customization and deliver individualized experiences at scale.

- **Integrating with Customer Data for Personalized Content**: Future DAMs will be more closely integrated with customer data platforms, enabling content personalization based on user behavior, preferences, and demographics. By linking assets in the DAM with customer segments, marketers can deliver content that resonates with specific audience groups, improving engagement.
- **AI-Driven Content Recommendations**: AI-powered DAMs can suggest content based on previous asset performance, audience segments, or campaign goals, making it easier to select high-impact visuals and messaging. These systems can analyze

historical data to predict which assets are likely to perform well with specific audiences, guiding personalization efforts.
- **Dynamic Asset Delivery**: Some DAMs are evolving to enable real-time asset customization, where content is dynamically assembled or adapted for each viewer. For instance, an e-commerce site could display personalized product images or promotional banners based on the customer's past purchases, browsing history, or geographic location, with all content managed directly through the DAM.

Example: Dynamic Personalization for an E-Commerce Brand

An e-commerce brand integrates their DAM with a customer data platform to dynamically serve personalized product images to returning customers. When a user who frequently shops for outdoor gear visits the website, the DAM delivers tailored product images and promotions, enhancing the shopping experience and driving conversions.

17.3 Facilitating Real-Time Content Creation and Distribution

In the fast-paced digital marketing world, the ability to create, adapt, and distribute content in real time has become essential. DAM systems are increasingly supporting real-time content needs by enabling streamlined workflows, collaborative tools, and automated distribution capabilities, allowing teams to move from concept to deployment faster than ever.

- **Collaborative Creation Tools**: Future DAMs are likely to include advanced collaboration tools that enable real-time asset editing and annotation, reducing back-and-forth between teams. With cloud-based access, creatives, marketers, and stakeholders can work together in the DAM, reviewing and refining assets as a group, which speeds up content creation and approval.
- **Automated Workflows for Faster Approvals**: Automated workflows with role-based approvals ensure that assets move smoothly through the review process, reducing bottlenecks and ensuring timely deployment. Notifications and reminders keep everyone on track, allowing assets to be reviewed, approved, and deployed in a fraction of the time.
- **Instant Content Distribution Across Channels**: As DAMs integrate more closely with CMS, social media platforms, and advertising tools, real-time distribution will become increasingly automated. This means that as soon as an asset is approved, it can be deployed instantly to the relevant channels, enabling real-time updates and campaigns that respond to current events or customer behaviors.

Example: Real-Time Content Deployment for a News Organization

A news organization uses a DAM with automated workflows and CMS integration to distribute breaking news graphics across their website, app, and social media channels instantly. As soon as graphics are approved, the DAM pushes them live, keeping the news feed current and relevant.

17.4 Leveraging AI and Automation for Predictive Content Planning

AI and machine learning are transforming how DAMs support content planning and strategy by providing predictive insights into asset performance, seasonal trends, and audience preferences. These insights help marketers make data-driven content decisions, improving campaign relevance and impact.

- **Predictive Analytics for Content Needs**: AI-driven DAMs can analyze historical data to predict content needs for future campaigns. By understanding which assets are typically in demand during specific seasons or events, marketers can prepare content in advance, aligning with audience interests.
- **Content Performance Forecasting**: Machine learning algorithms can analyze past campaign performance to forecast which assets are likely to succeed in upcoming campaigns. By recommending high-impact visuals, these systems help marketers make strategic choices that maximize engagement and ROI.
- **Automated Content Refresh Recommendations**: Some DAMs are beginning to offer content refresh suggestions, automatically

identifying assets that may benefit from updates based on their age, past performance, or relevance to new campaigns. This feature keeps content fresh and aligned with current trends without manual oversight.

Example: Predictive Content Planning for a Travel Brand

A travel brand uses a DAM with predictive analytics to identify high-performing images for seasonal campaigns. Based on past data, the DAM suggests which destination photos are most likely to engage audiences during peak vacation months, helping the marketing team prioritize assets that drive conversions.

17.5 Preparing for Advanced Integrations and Emerging Technologies

The future of DAM will also be defined by its ability to integrate with emerging technologies and advanced tools, such as augmented reality (AR), virtual reality (VR), and blockchain for rights management. Staying informed about these advancements allows organizations to be ready for future shifts in content creation and distribution.

- **Augmented Reality (AR) and Virtual Reality (VR)**: As AR and VR become more popular, DAMs will need to support these asset types, providing storage, organization, and version control for 3D models, virtual environments, and interactive content. This will open new possibilities for immersive brand experiences.

- **Blockchain for Rights Management**: Blockchain can provide an unalterable record of asset ownership, usage rights, and licensing terms. Future DAMs may leverage blockchain technology to enforce rights automatically, restricting unauthorized use and providing transparent tracking for high-value assets.
- **Advanced Integrations with Martech and Analytics Platforms**: Future-ready DAMs will offer more seamless integrations with other martech tools, such as customer data platforms (CDPs), AI-driven recommendation engines, and advanced analytics platforms. These integrations enable organizations to leverage their DAM as a central hub for personalized, data-driven content strategies.

Example: AR Integration for a Real Estate Company

A real estate company integrates their DAM with an AR platform to store and manage 3D property models, allowing users to experience virtual property tours on their mobile devices. The DAM ensures all models are accessible, current, and aligned with the company's brand standards.

Conclusion

The future of DAM is dynamic, adaptive, and deeply integrated with emerging technologies. As organizations prepare for the next generation of multi-channel marketing, dynamic personalization, and real-time content creation, DAMs will play a crucial role in delivering timely, relevant, and engaging content to diverse audiences. By embracing AI, predictive analytics, and advanced integrations, organizations can future-proof their DAMs, ensuring they remain valuable, versatile, and aligned with evolving business needs. Preparing for these advancements allows your organization to stay ahead, leveraging DAM as a strategic tool that enhances agility, efficiency, and impact.

With this understanding of future trends, your organization is well-positioned to adapt to the next evolution in content management, using DAM to support both current and emerging marketing strategies.

Chapter 18: Emerging DAM Use Cases and What Marketers Should Expect

Predicting new applications of DAM in marketing, such as shoppable assets, immersive experiences, and AI-driven content creation.

TL;DR

Emerging DAM use cases are transforming how marketers create, deploy, and optimize content. DAM systems are evolving to support shoppable assets that drive conversions directly within images and videos, immersive experiences with AR and VR, and AI-driven content creation that automates and personalizes visuals. New capabilities also

include managing interactive and gamified content, enabling real-time content deployment during live events, and enhancing rights management with tools like blockchain and AI for automated compliance. By preparing for these advancements, marketers can leverage DAM to deliver engaging, personalized, and compliant content across a rapidly evolving digital landscape.

As digital marketing continues to innovate, new applications for Digital Asset Management (DAM) systems are emerging, driven by advances in technology, shifts in consumer behavior, and the growing demand for immersive and interactive experiences. Beyond traditional asset storage and management, DAMs are beginning to support shoppable content, immersive experiences like augmented reality (AR) and virtual reality (VR), and AI-powered content creation and adaptation. In this chapter, we'll explore these emerging DAM use cases and discuss how they're likely to shape the future of marketing, allowing organizations to create more engaging, personalized, and efficient content experiences.

18.1 Shoppable Assets for E-Commerce and Social Media

As e-commerce and social media continue to converge, shoppable assets are becoming a powerful tool for driving conversions directly within digital content. DAM systems are evolving to support this trend, enabling marketers to manage and deploy assets embedded with shopping capabilities, making the path from discovery to purchase as seamless as possible.

- **Managing Shoppable Content Across Channels**: DAMs can organize and store shoppable assets, allowing marketers to maintain consistency across platforms such as Instagram, Pinterest, and in-app advertisements. With shoppable tags and links, customers can purchase products directly from visual content, reducing friction in the customer journey.
- **Creating Shoppable Variants for Different Audiences**: With DAM, marketers can store different versions of shoppable assets tailored to specific demographics or regions. For example, a clothing retailer can use their DAM to manage assets with localized pricing, seasonal adjustments, or curated product selections.
- **Tracking Shoppable Content Performance**: Integrating shoppable content with analytics tools allows DAMs to capture data on customer interactions, clicks, and conversions. This data helps marketers refine their strategies by identifying which assets drive the highest engagement and revenue.

Example: Shoppable Content for a Fashion Brand

A fashion brand uses its DAM to store and manage shoppable images for their seasonal collections. By embedding links in product photos shared across social media, email newsletters, and their website, customers can click directly from the image to the purchase page, streamlining the buying process and increasing conversions.

18.2 Supporting Immersive Experiences with AR and VR

Immersive experiences, such as augmented reality (AR) and virtual reality (VR), are changing the way consumers interact with brands, allowing them to explore products and environments in a more engaging and interactive way. DAM systems are evolving to store, manage, and deploy 3D assets, making it easier for marketers to incorporate AR and VR into their campaigns.

- **Storing and Organizing 3D and Interactive Assets**: Future DAMs will increasingly support 3D models, VR environments, and AR-enabled assets, allowing marketers to manage these files as easily as traditional images and videos. By categorizing and tagging 3D content, DAMs make it easy to locate and deploy assets for immersive experiences.
- **Integrating with AR/VR Platforms**: DAMs integrated with AR and VR platforms enable seamless content deployment, allowing assets to be used in applications, online environments, or physical spaces. This integration simplifies the process of creating interactive experiences for events, e-commerce, or social media.
- **Personalizing Immersive Experiences**: As DAMs connect with customer data platforms, marketers can create personalized AR or VR experiences. For example, customers could view a virtual

room with products that match their previous purchases or preferences, creating a unique and engaging experience.

Example: AR-Enhanced Shopping for a Home Decor Company

A home decor company stores 3D furniture models in their DAM, which are then used to create AR-enabled shopping experiences. Customers can place virtual furniture in their own spaces using a mobile app, allowing them to visualize products before buying. The DAM organizes and manages these assets, making it easy to deploy updates as new products are released.

18.3 AI-Driven Content Creation and Adaptation

AI transforms how content is created, personalized, and adapted, allowing DAM systems to support automated content generation and customization at scale. With AI-powered tools, DAMs can help marketers produce assets more efficiently and tailor them for individual audiences.

- **Automated Image and Video Editing**: AI-powered DAMs can assist with basic editing tasks like cropping, resizing, and filtering, allowing marketers to quickly generate different versions of an asset. This automation speeds up the content creation process and ensures that assets meet the specifications of each platform.

- **Dynamic Content Generation**: Some DAMs are integrating generative AI capabilities, enabling marketers to create entirely new images, videos, or even written content based on pre-set parameters. For example, a DAM could generate a new ad visual with different backgrounds, colors, or text options based on campaign needs.
- **Personalized Asset Adaptation**: AI in DAMs can analyze user data to create personalized versions of content. For instance, a DAM might automatically generate different product image variants for users in different geographic locations, ensuring that content feels relevant and culturally appropriate.

Example: AI-Powered Content Adaptation for a Global Retailer

A global retailer uses AI-driven adaptation in their DAM to localize product images for different regions. The DAM automatically changes backgrounds, currencies, and models to match regional preferences, enabling the brand to deliver localized content efficiently across multiple markets.

18.4 Enabling Interactive and Gamified Content

Interactive and gamified content—such as quizzes, polls, and mini-games—engages consumers by inviting them to participate rather than passively consuming content. DAM systems increasingly support interactive assets that allow marketers to create more engaging brand experiences.

- **Managing Interactive Assets**: Future DAMs will enable marketers to store and manage interactive assets like quizzes, polls, and drag-and-drop features. By organizing these assets with relevant metadata, DAMs make it easy for marketers to find and deploy interactive content across campaigns.
- **Connecting with Gamification Platforms**: Integrations with gamification platforms allow DAMs to support interactive experiences designed to boost engagement and retention. Marketers can leverage these assets on websites, apps, and social media to foster deeper audience connections.
- **Tracking Engagement and Insights**: With analytics integrations, DAMs can capture data on user interactions with interactive content, helping marketers understand what resonates with audiences. Insights from interactive assets can guide content strategies and reveal opportunities for further engagement.

Example: Gamified Marketing for an Automotive Brand

An automotive brand uses its DAM to store interactive quiz assets that help potential customers find the right car model based on their preferences. This gamified experience is embedded on the brand's website and shared via social media, creating a fun, personalized journey that leads customers toward purchase.

18.5 Leveraging DAM for Real-Time Marketing and Event Activation

In fast-paced marketing environments, delivering content in real time is essential, especially for live events, product launches, and seasonal campaigns. DAM systems are evolving to support real-time content distribution, ensuring assets are available when needed.

- **Instant Content Deployment for Live Events**: DAMs integrated with content management and social media platforms allow marketers to instantly deploy approved assets to multiple channels during live events. This capability helps brands maintain momentum and engage audiences in the moment.
- **Real-Time Content Adaptation**: AI-driven DAMs can dynamically update assets based on real-time data, such as audience engagement, weather, or location. This adaptation allows brands to provide timely, relevant content during live campaigns, keeping audiences engaged.
- **Supporting Real-Time Data Feeds**: As DAMs integrate with real-time data feeds, marketers can create content that reacts to current events, trends, or user behaviors. For example, a DAM could automatically pull in live social media feeds or event footage, creating content that is always fresh and engaging.

Example: Real-Time Marketing for a Sports Brand

A sports brand leverages real-time content deployment during major athletic events. Their DAM is connected to social media and their website, allowing them to instantly release event images, athlete profiles, and highlight videos as the event unfolds. This strategy keeps the brand's audience engaged and amplifies their real-time marketing reach.

18.6 Enhanced Rights Management and Compliance

With the proliferation of digital content, managing rights and compliance is increasingly complex. Future DAMs will leverage advanced tools like blockchain and AI to provide transparent, automated rights management, ensuring that assets are used legally and ethically.

- **Blockchain for Rights Verification**: Blockchain technology allows DAMs to provide a transparent, unchangeable record of asset ownership and usage rights. By leveraging blockchain, DAMs can automatically verify that assets meet licensing and usage requirements before deployment.
- **AI-Powered Compliance Checks**: AI-driven DAMs can automate compliance by scanning assets for potential issues, such as expired licenses or inappropriate content for certain regions. These tools help marketers deploy assets confidently, knowing they meet all necessary regulations.
- **Automated Licensing and Expiration Alerts**: DAMs equipped with automated alert systems can notify users when asset licenses

are about to expire or need renewal. This feature helps avoid legal risks and ensures that only compliant assets are in use.

Example: Rights Management for a Publishing Company

A publishing company uses blockchain-based rights management in their DAM to track image licenses and usage rights for international editions. The DAM provides a transparent record of asset ownership and automatically flags any content that needs license renewal, reducing compliance risks.

Conclusion

As DAM technology advances, marketers have new opportunities to leverage it for emerging use cases like shoppable content, immersive experiences, AI-driven content creation, and interactive and real-time marketing. Future DAMs will enable brands to create more personalized, engaging, and compliant content across channels. By staying informed about these trends and preparing to integrate these capabilities, organizations can ensure their DAM remains a vital, strategic asset in the fast-evolving digital landscape.

Epilogue

Digital Asset Management (DAM) has evolved far beyond a basic storage solution, becoming an essential tool for enhancing marketing efficiency, creativity, and impact. By centralizing assets, streamlining workflows, and integrating with other marketing technologies, DAM empowers teams to deliver consistent, high-quality content across channels—fast. Throughout this guide, we've explored how DAM can elevate marketing efforts, from supporting multi-channel campaigns to enabling dynamic personalization, real-time content deployment, and emerging use cases like shoppable assets and immersive experiences.

The key takeaways for leveraging DAM as a competitive advantage are clear: effective implementation, consistent organization, and ongoing optimization are essential to maximizing DAM's potential. Implementing best practices—such as robust governance, regular evaluations, and continuous training—ensures that DAM remains a valuable resource that scales with your organization. As DAM technology advances, integrating features like AI-driven personalization, interactive content support, and enhanced rights management opens exciting new possibilities for engaging customers and maintaining brand integrity.

Looking ahead, marketers should view DAM as more than a tool—it's a strategic asset that can transform how you approach content. By applying these best practices and staying attuned to emerging capabilities, you can ensure that your DAM continues to drive innovation, agility, and impact in your marketing strategy, setting your organization apart in a competitive digital landscape.

Also, make sure to stay tuned to The Agile Brand Guide website, where we have podcasts, articles, and wiki items that relate to this important aspect of your marketing work.

Until next time, stay agile!

Appendix 1: DAM Evaluation Checklist

Here's a detailed DAM Evaluation Checklist with three rating levels: **Poor**, **Fair**, and **Good** for each evaluation criteria. While your unique case might have some specific criteria, this type of evaluation has proven helpful in many evaluations. Feel free to add or remove items that are a good fit (or not).

Evaluation Criteria	Description	Rating (1 - poor, 2 - Fair, 3 - Good)

User Interface	Is the interface intuitive and user-friendly?	
Search Functionality	Can users easily search, filter, and locate assets?	
Metadata Management	Does the DAM support robust metadata tagging and management?	
AI-Powered Features	Are AI tools available for tagging, facial recognition, or recommendations?	
Asset Versioning	Is version control available and easy to use?	
Access Control & Permissions	Are there flexible permission settings to control access based on roles?	
Workflow Automation	Does the DAM support automation of repetitive tasks, such as approval processes or metadata tagging?	

File Support & Compatibility	Is the DAM compatible with various file formats (images, videos, documents, etc.)?	
Multi-Channel Distribution	Can assets be distributed across multiple platforms from within the DAM?	
Integrations	Does the DAM integrate well with other tools in the marketing stack (e.g., CMS, CRM, project management)?	
Mobile Access	Is the DAM accessible and functional on mobile devices?	
Security Features	Are there sufficient security features, such as DRM, watermarking, and secure access protocols?	
Scalability	Can the DAM scale as the volume of assets grows?	

Taxonomy & Folder Structure	Is there flexibility to organize assets with a logical taxonomy and folder structure?	
Reporting & Analytics	Does the DAM offer reporting and analytics on asset usage, performance, and user activity?	
Asset Preview Options	Are high-quality previews available for different asset types?	
Collaboration Features	Does the DAM enable team collaboration, such as comments, approvals, or shared workspaces?	
Support for Brand Guidelines	Can brand guidelines be enforced through the DAM to maintain consistency?	
Support for Custom Workflows	Are custom workflows for asset approvals, edits, and publishing supported?	

Ease of Onboarding	Is the DAM easy to set up, configure, and onboard new users?	
Training and Support Resources	Does the provider offer sufficient training and support resources (e.g., guides, tutorials, customer support)?	
Cost-Effectiveness	Is the DAM's pricing reasonable for the features and value provided?	
User Roles and Permissions	Can roles and permissions be customized to suit different user types?	
API Access	Is there API access for custom integrations and flexibility?	
Data Migration Tools	Are there tools or support available to facilitate data migration into the DAM?	
Ongoing Software Updates	Are regular updates provided to keep the DAM current with new features and	

	security patches?	
Digital Rights Management (DRM)	Does the DAM provide DRM to manage and protect asset usage rights?	
Compliance with Industry Standards	Is the DAM compliant with industry standards (e.g., GDPR, CCPA for privacy)?	

This table provides a straightforward, easy-to-use checklist for marketers to evaluate DAM systems across critical features, with clear rating options to assess each one. Let me know if you'd like any additional categories or specific examples!

Appendix 2: Glossary of Digital Asset Management (DAM) Terms

1. Access Control
The process of defining and managing permissions for users and groups within a DAM. Access control settings allow administrators to restrict or grant access to certain assets based on roles or user privileges.

2. AI Tagging
The use of artificial intelligence to automatically assign metadata to assets, such as keywords, categories, and visual features, making it easier to search and organize content.

3. API (Application Programming Interface)
A set of protocols that allows different software applications to

communicate with each other. In DAM, APIs enable integration with other marketing tools like CMS, CRM, or social media platforms.

4. Asset Lifecycle

The various stages an asset goes through from creation to archiving or deletion. Key stages include creation, approval, distribution, usage, and retirement.

5. Asset Versioning

A feature that manages different versions of an asset, allowing users to revert to a previous version if needed. Versioning helps maintain consistency and track changes over time.

6. Batch Processing

The ability to perform actions on multiple assets simultaneously, such as uploading, tagging, or applying permissions, which improves efficiency.

7. Brand Guidelines

Rules and standards that ensure consistent use of branding elements (e.g., logos, colors, fonts) across all assets. DAM systems often include tools to enforce these guidelines.

8. Cloud-Based DAM

A DAM hosted on the cloud, offering flexibility, scalability, and remote access. Cloud-based DAM solutions reduce the need for on-premises infrastructure and allow for easier collaboration.

9. CMS (Content Management System)

A platform used to manage, publish, and organize digital content, typically on websites. DAM systems often integrate with CMS platforms to streamline asset distribution.

10. Content Personalization

The customization of content based on user preferences, behavior, or demographics. DAM systems support personalization by storing assets tagged for specific audiences or channels.

11. DAM Governance

The policies, roles, and procedures for managing and maintaining a DAM system. Governance includes rules for asset management, user roles, security, and compliance.

12. Data Migration

The process of transferring digital assets from one storage solution to another, such as when moving assets into a new DAM. This can involve reformatting, re-tagging, or cleaning data.

13. DRM (Digital Rights Management)

A technology that controls how digital assets are used, distributed, and accessed. DRM features in DAM ensure compliance with copyright and licensing requirements.

14. Facial Recognition

An AI feature that identifies faces in images, allowing for easier categorization and retrieval of photos involving specific people.

15. Folder Structure

The organizational hierarchy within a DAM where assets are stored. A well-designed folder structure aids in asset discoverability and minimizes search time.

16. Keyword Tagging

A metadata process where keywords are manually or automatically assigned to an asset. Keywords enhance searchability within the DAM by providing relevant search terms.

17. Metadata

Data that describes other data, providing information about an asset's content, such as title, author, creation date, and keywords. Metadata is essential for efficient asset management and retrieval.

18. Multi-Channel Distribution

The ability to distribute assets across multiple channels (e.g., social media, email, websites) directly from the DAM. This feature simplifies cross-channel content marketing.

19. On-Premises DAM

A DAM system that is hosted and managed within an organization's own IT infrastructure, offering more control but often requiring more resources for maintenance.

20. Permissions

Settings that define what actions a user or group can take within the DAM. Permissions may include viewing, editing, downloading, or deleting assets.

21. Role-Based Access Control (RBAC)

A system that assigns access rights to users based on their roles within an organization. RBAC ensures users only access the assets relevant to their role.

22. SEO (Search Engine Optimization)

The practice of optimizing content to improve its visibility on search engines. DAM systems often help by ensuring assets are tagged with SEO-friendly metadata.

23. Taxonomy

The structured categorization of assets within a DAM, using hierarchical tags or categories. A well-planned taxonomy simplifies asset search and retrieval.

24. Thumbnails

Small, low-resolution previews of assets displayed within the DAM. Thumbnails provide a quick visual reference to identify assets without needing to open them.

25. User Permissions

Settings that control which users can access, view, edit, or share specific assets within the DAM, based on their role or user level.

26. Version Control

A feature that tracks changes to an asset, allowing users to access and restore previous versions if needed. Version control is useful for managing edits and updates to content over time.

27. Watermarking

A security feature that adds a visible overlay (e.g., logo or text) to an asset to indicate ownership or prevent unauthorized use.

28. Workflow Automation

The use of automated processes within the DAM to manage the lifecycle of assets, such as approval, tagging, or archiving. Workflow automation improves efficiency and ensures consistency.

29. XML (Extensible Markup Language)

A flexible data format commonly used to structure data, including metadata in a DAM system. XML supports interoperability and data sharing between different platforms.

30. XMP (Extensible Metadata Platform)

A standard for embedding metadata into digital files, making it easier to organize and manage assets within a DAM system.

www.ingramcontent.com/pod-product-compliance
Lightning Source LLC
Chambersburg PA
CBHW071452220526
45472CB00003B/771